W9-BOA-123

WHAT WORKS

Research About Teaching and Learning

United States Department of Education
William J. Bennett, Secretary
1986

THE WHITE HOUSE

WASHINGTON

January 30, 1986

We Americans have always considered education a
key to individual achievement and national strength.
We know that education begins in the home and
flourishes when it draws upon the combined efforts
of children, parents, teachers, and administrators.

What Works provides practical knowledge to help
in the education of our children. In assembling
some of the best available research for use by
the American public, What Works exemplifies the
type of information the Federal government can
and should provide.

I am confident that with the benefit of such
knowledge and renewed trust in common sense, we
Americans will have even greater success in our
unstinting efforts to improve our schools and better
prepare our children for the challenges of today's
world.

Ronald Reagan

FOREWORD

William J. Bennett
Secretary of Education

*U*nlike many government reports, this report is addressed to the American people. It is intended to provide accurate and reliable information about *what works* in the education of our children, and it is meant to be useful to all of us—parents and taxpayers, teachers and legislators, newspaper reporters and newspaper readers, principals and school board members. But, first and foremost, this book is intended to be useful to the adult with a child—or grandchild, niece, stepchild, neighbor—in school or soon to enter school. It is designed to assist the adult who cares about the education of that child, both at home and in school.

The preparation of this report has been in my mind since the day, a year ago, when I was sworn in as Secretary of Education. In my first statement upon assuming this office, I said, "We must remember that education is not a dismal science. In education research, of course, there is much to find out, but education, despite efforts to make it so, is not essentially mysterious." In an interview shortly thereafter, I added that "I hope we can make sense about education and talk sense about education in terms that the American public can understand. I would like to demystify a lot of things that don't need to be mystifying. I would like specifically to have the best information available to the Department and therefore to the American people...."

The first and fundamental responsibility of the federal government in the field of education is to supply accurate and reliable information about education to the American people. The information in this volume is a distillation of a large body of scholarly research in the field of education. I trust it is a useful distillation. Of course, it is a selective one. It consists of discrete findings about teaching and learning that are applicable at home, in the classroom, and in the school. Many larger policy questions, many important education issues, are not addressed in this volume. And research on other important issues that could have been addressed was judged too preliminary or tentative to be included. But we now *know* certain things about teaching and learning as a result of the labors of the scholarly community. This book makes available to the American people a synthesis of some of that knowledge about education.

Primary responsibility for assembling the material in this report has been borne by Dr. Chester E. Finn, Jr., Assistant Secretary for Research and Improvement, and his staff. Immediately after Dr. Finn took his oath of office, I assigned him the preparation of this document as his first task. As he explains in the brief introduction that follows, many have contributed their ideas, knowledge, and energies, and I am grateful to them all. Beyond these individuals, though, we all have cause to be grateful to the scholarly community whose research is distilled here. We salute their accomplishments by paying them the highest possible compliment: taking their work seriously and trying to make it accessible to the American people. Many readers may find some of the research findings surprising. Most readers will, I think, judge that most of the evidence in this volume confirms common sense. So be it. Given the abuse common sense has taken in recent decades, particularly in the theory and practice of education, it is no small contribution if research can play a role in bringing more of it to American education. Indeed, the reinforcement these findings give to common sense should bolster our confidence that we, as a people, can act together to improve our schools.

I for one am confident that the American people are ready, willing, and able to improve their schools, and to assist their children to learn. The principal contribution that the federal government can make is to supply good information to the American people as they embark on this endeavor. Armed with good information, the American people can be trusted to fix their own schools. As this report makes clear, there is also much they can do at home.

This volume is not the only effort that the Department of Education is making to supply the American people with important, accurate, and useful information. We publish regular data compilations, such as the annual *Condition of Education*. We have produced pamphlets explaining to par-

ents what parents can do to assist their children to acquire some of the basic academic skills. We have supported work by others that has yielded such exemplary reports as *Becoming a Nation of Readers* (the Report of the Commission on Reading, many of whose findings and conclusions are cited in this volume).

Nor do we intend to stop. I would, in fact, welcome suggestions for future efforts that would be helpful and informative, as well as comments and criticisms about this volume. And please use the comment card inside the back cover of this volume to pose questions about education not addressed in this report. For now, I am pleased to offer this volume to the American people. I believe that it represents an important step toward fulfilling the mandate of Congress, dating back to 1867, that the federal government should provide information to the people of the United States so as to "promote the cause of education throughout the country."

WHAT WORKS

*Research
About
Teaching
and
Learning*

CONTENTS

INTRODUCTION

> *Badness you can get easily, in quantity: the road is smooth, and it lies close by. But in front of excellence the immortal gods have put sweat, and long and steep is the way to it, and rough at first. But when you come to the top, then it is easy, even though it is hard.*
>
> Hesiod, c. 700 B.C.
> *The Theogony*

Chester E. Finn, Jr.
Assistant Secretary for
Research and Improvement

*A*s Secretary Bennett notes in his foreword, preparing this volume was the first assignment that I received when I joined him at the Department of Education in June 1985, just as restructuring and streamlining the part of the Department that produces research and statistics was the first major "organizational" effort that Dr. Bennett launched after assuming his present office.

What is the message in these two actions? They show that we believe strongly in the responsibility of the Department of Education to gather information and generate knowledge about education in an efficient and energetic manner and then *make that information and knowledge accessible to people who might benefit from them.*

But it turns out to be easier to gather data and support research than to make results available in forms that people will find clear and useful. Statistical data tend to come in vast, indigestible quantities, often without the markers of changes and trends, improvements and declines, that distinguish information that is merely interesting from that which can form the basis for decisions and actions. As for research findings, scholars ordinarily write for other scholars and they seldom know as much as they think they should know before drawing definite conclusions. In many research areas, furthermore, there are conflicts between rival interpretations of the same evidence, and at every turn conclusions are hedged by the well-known academic caution: statistical correlation does not reliably indicate causation. Finally, scholars and laymen are often at odds about the significance of things. What strikes the scholar as interesting and important may seem to the layman remote and trivial; what

the layman wants most to know may strike the researcher as banal, simplistic, or vague.

Despite yeoman efforts, we may yet stumble into some of those traps between the covers of this slim volume. We may present research findings that some readers will find obscure, puzzling, or impracticable and still others that seem to be oversimplifications of complex phenomena or premature resolutions of hotly contested disputes.

This risk we must take, but we have tried to minimize it. The book does not make a particular point, beyond the straightforward one that education is susceptible both to being understood and to being improved. We have provided evidence from many but not all spheres of education research. We sought findings that, in Secretary Bennett's frequent phrase, are "true, useful and important." We included only those findings about which research evidence and expert opinion were consistent, persuasive, and fairly stable over time. Each finding in this volume has been checked and rechecked by professional staff members in the Office of Educational Research and Improvement and by expert outside reviewers. During this process, we discarded more items than we kept, among them dozens of research findings that we judged to be less reliable, less helpful, or less consequential than those we retained.

It must also be noted that people do not necessarily agree about what knowledge is most useful or important. They may even disagree about what is "known," sometimes because the evidence is mixed, sometimes because one may not welcome the implication of another's "knowledge." Statistical significance aside, since what is certain to one may be inconclusive to

1

another, we have tried to follow the wisdom of Socrates who explained (to Meno, in Plato's dialogue of that name) that "true opinion is as good a guide to correct action as knowledge." Solid knowledge is surely to be preferred, but to wait for absolute certainty is sometimes to wait too long, particularly in the field of education where millions of children are affected every day by our actions. If we would have those actions be as well-informed as possible, in situations where we do not have knowledge we can reasonably allow our actions to be informed by "true opinion," by what informed people judge to be the "most likely story." In this volume, as you will see, we draw upon the knowledge and opinions both of modern scholars and of distinguished thinkers of earlier times.

Let me now take up several questions to which readers may want answers.

Is this report comprehensive?

No. In many branches of education that people regard as important, not much formal research has yet been done, or that which has been done is fragmentary, inconclusive, or hotly disputed. A substantial portion of educational research is of relatively recent vintage, and much that has been done in the past several decades has centered around this straightforward question: What can we do to make it more likely that all children will emerge into adulthood with the basic skills and knowledge that some children routinely seem to acquire as they pass from home through elementary and secondary school? Because variations on that question have—I think properly—driven so much of our research to date, we should not be surprised that we have learned relatively more about it. But that means less attention has thus far been devoted to other issues in education that also deserve study.

Why do so many of these findings look so obvious? Was "research" really needed to reveal what intuition and common sense would show?

In the absence of reliable and valid evidence or experience, our unprejudiced views are usually shaped by intuition and common sense. Until they are put to the test, however, one person's intuition and common sense are as reliable—or unreliable—as another's, and they are often in conflict. In company with some geographers and scientists of his day, Columbus surmised that the world was round. But many less astute observers embraced the conventional wisdom of his time and insisted that it was flat; this "wisdom" did not change until Columbus tested the true opinion of himself and the scientists with the voyage that discovered America and *proved* their version of the truth to be correct.

In education, too, research sometimes appears to confirm the self-evident. But sometimes it raises important doubts about conventional wisdom.

Why is so much of the research about elementary schools and disadvantaged children?

This situation stems from the ambitious educational reforms of the 1960's. Ironically, it is also one more example of the failings of conventional wisdom. Two decades ago, conventional wisdom about education held that disadvantaged and minority children did poorly in school mainly because of the inequitable distribution of educational resources. To document this belief, Congress commissioned a huge national survey of the schools. The resulting project came to be known as the Coleman Report. This was probably the best known and most influential piece of educational research ever published. Its conclusion that unequal achievement could *not* be ascribed to unequal school resources so offended the conventional wisdom of the time that the next 20 years of educational research have been dominated by the quest for contrary evidence. But, of course, the problem of educational disadvantage—a problem still with us today—was deeper and more complex than any simple disparity in the size of school libraries or the condition of school buildings. Its roots reached into the home and the classroom. Coleman's discovery, for example, that there was more difference in the achievement of black children *within* the same school than from one school to another also led researchers to examine more closely the interaction between teacher and student rather than just the effects of school facilities, spending levels, or class size.

This line of inquiry is visible throughout the past two decades of educational research, much of which describes practices found to be particularly effective in fostering the academic education of disadvantaged school children. Heated arguments about the appropriate expectations and methods of instruction for disadvantaged children were commonplace during the 1960's and 1970's. Research had to document common sense: children are more likely to learn the basics in schools that emphasize the basics and less likely to learn them in schools that do not.

It has been a worthy effort. The critical features of instruction and organization for more effective schools were documented by research. (A number of them are summarized and repeated

in this volume.) It is no coincidence that the achievement scores of disadvantaged elementary school students have steadily improved in the past decades. That part of the academic puzzle has been at least partly demystified.

Would all children benefit equally from the application of the facts and findings contained in this report?

Within the range and limits of the evidence, we have tried to deal with the "general" or "usual" or "average" situation, not with all the special circumstances that are found among millions of children, tens of thousands of schools, and thousands of school systems in as many communities. Hence no one will find here a map out of every tangled situation or a solution to each distinctive problem. In an enterprise as large and variegated as American education, many children, teachers, parents, and schools differ from the "general" in various respects. But few differ in all respects and we therefore hope that practically everyone will find something of interest and relevance in the pages that follow.

Why does the report contain so few specific recommendations about actions that should be taken?

This is not an education "cookbook" so much as a "guide to sound nutrition." Specific policies, practices, and actions are the responsibility of the parent and the school, the teacher and principal, the school board and the State. The appropriate design and implementation of these policies, practices, and actions will differ according to local conditions and it is not the place of the federal government to interfere. Nor do we seek to exhort people to do anything that contradicts their own "true opinions," although we would urge you to subject them to the

3

test of experience at every opportunity. The purpose of this volume is to provide reliable information that people can, if they wish, put to use in various ways. In most instances, the reader will rapidly be able to visualize some implications for action of findings that we have included.

Why are so many of these findings aimed at parents and teachers rather than at those who direct and make policy for the "education system?"

Let us emphasize that many of them are indeed meant for *parents* as well as for professional teachers. Parents are the child's first and most influential teachers. If parents are not effective teachers, then in most cases the school will have far greater difficulty being effective.

As for administrators and policymakers, we believe that they, too, will find in this volume many implications —if not specific recommendations— for their own activities. Besides setting overall standards and furnishing resources, perhaps their most important function is to create the conditions in which parents and teachers, working together, can maximize their own educational effectiveness.

What of the students themselves? Don't they share in this responsibility?

Indeed, yes. The passive learner usually doesn't learn much and the hostile student rarely learns anything worthwhile. Many of the findings in this volume convey—or assume—an old-fashioned "desire for improvement" on the part of the child; others indicate the sorts of actions that parents or teachers can take to maximize the child's enthusiasm for learning and to avoid chilling his ardor.

While it is true that some children have difficulty mastering complicated subjects, few are without resources to do so. More commonly, the resources they have are underused. Parents can play vital and constructive roles in the education of their own children, and research has illuminated sound methods of home assistance. Students can add greatly to the time provided in school with time set aside at home for study and other forms of homework. We see too little "self-help" in many households today, especially among those students whose academic achievement is lagging and who need it the most.

What if I want to learn more than this volume contains?

To assist the reader interested in more evidence or in exploring the actual research, each finding is accompanied by citations of several sources for further reading. Most of these sources can be obtained through a good library. In turn, many of those citations lead to articles, books, or studies that contain lengthy bibliographies of their own. We did not try to provide complete research documentation, but in every instance we have pointed the direction to further—and deeper—understanding. In addition, we would invite your attention to the Education Research Information Clearinghouse (ERIC) system, supported by the Department of Education, which provides extensive information about research findings and which can be accessed through most libraries.

This volume appears at a special time. American education is undergoing enormous reform, a nationwide effort to improve the outcomes of schooling and reverse the decline in student achievement that developed over the past quarter century. Many of the actors are new; for example, the governors of many States have taken a deep interest in the quality of schools and colleges in their jurisdictions, and many State legislatures have stolen the march on the education profession in prescribing the reforms that they expect will boost educational outcomes. The contents of this volume ought to be of help to them, as well as to parents, teachers, and citizens.

We do not, however, claim to be offering pat answers or simple nostrums. It is not reasonable to expect research to resolve all issues or to erase all differences of opinion. We can but supply some information that we think reliable and we will continue in the future to supply more. But it is up to the American people to decide what to do. The better their information, the wiser will be their decisions.

Finally, on behalf of Secretary Bennett as well as myself, I want to thank the many individuals whose efforts made this report possible.

Milton Goldberg and Jim Bencivenga were responsible for project oversight and management. Development and production of the material in this volume was accomplished through the extraordinary efforts of Tommy M. Tomlinson and Susan Traiman. Editing through many drafts was coordinated by Kay McKinney with major assistance from Laurie Maxwell. Several dozen staff members of the Office of Educational Research and Improvement also contributed to this project and their names appear at the end of the volume.

We especially appreciate the contributions of the outside reviewers who did their best to help assure the accuracy, veracity, validity, and importance of the contents of this report: Joseph Adelson, Lois Coit, Bernard R. Gifford, Robert Glaser, Robert Hogan, Michael Kirst, Rita Kramer, Leanna Landsmann, Jean Marzollo, and Diane Ravitch. Particular thanks are due to Professor Herbert Walberg for his manifold efforts on our behalf. While the Department of Education is properly responsible for any error of style, substance, or selection, the willing assistance of these reviewers has added immeasurably to the quality of the result.

HOME

If we want to educate a person in virtue we must polish him at a tender age. And if someone is to advance toward wisdom he must be opened up for it in the first years of his life when his industriousness is still burning, his mind is malleable, and his memory still strong.

Comenius, 1592-1670
The Great Didactic

Curriculum of the Home

Research Finding: **Parents are their children's first and most influential teachers. What parents do to help their children learn is more important to academic success than how well-off the family is.**

Comment: Parents can do many things at home to help their children succeed in school. Unfortunately, recent evidence indicates that many parents are doing much less than they might. For example, American mothers on average spend less than half an hour a day talking, explaining, or reading with their children. Fathers spend less than 15 minutes.

They can create a "curriculum of the home" that teaches their children what matters. They do this through their daily conversations, household routines, attention to school matters, and affectionate concern for their children's progress.

Conversation is important. Children learn to read, reason, and understand things better when their parents:
• read, talk, and listen to them,
• tell them stories, play games, share hobbies, and
• discuss news, TV programs, and special events.

In order to enrich the "curriculum of the home," some parents:
• provide books, supplies, and a special place for studying,
• observe routine for meals, bedtime, and homework, and
• monitor the amount of time spent watching TV and doing after-school jobs.

Parents stay aware of their children's lives at school when they:
• discuss school events,
• help children meet deadlines, and
• talk with their children about school problems and successes.

Research on both gifted and disadvantaged children shows that home efforts can greatly improve student achievement. For example, when parents of disadvantaged children take the steps listed above, their children can do as well at school as the children of more affluent families.

References:

DiPrete, T. A. (1981). *Discipline, Order, and Student Behavior in American High Schools.* Chicago: National Opinion Research Center. ERIC Document No. ED 224137.

Graue, M. E., Weinstein, T., and Walberg, H. J. (1983). "School-based Home Instruction and Learning: A Quantitative Synthesis." *Journal of Educational Research*, Vol. 76, pp. 351-360.

Gray, S. T. (1984). "How to Create a Successful School/Community Partnership." *Phi Delta Kappan*, Vol. 65, No. 6, pp. 405-409.

Walberg, H. J. (1984). "Families as Partners in Educational Productivity." *Phi Delta Kappan*, Vol. 65, No. 6, pp. 397-400.

Walberg, H. J. (1984). "Improving the Productivity of America's Schools." *Educational Leadership*, Vol. 41, No. 8, pp. 19-27.

*When by these gentle ways
[a child] begins to be able to
read, some easy pleasant book,
suited to his capacity, should be
put into his hands, wherein the
entertainment that he finds,
might draw him on, and reward
his pains in reading; and yet
not such as should fill his head
with perfectly useless trumpery,
or lay the principles of vice and
folly. To this purpose I think
Aesop's Fables the best, which
being stories apt to delight and
entertain a child, may yet
afford useful reflections to a
grown man; and if his memory
retain them all his life after, he
will not repent to find them
there, amongst his manly
thoughts, and serious business.*

John Locke, 1632-1704
Some Thoughts on Education

Reading to Children

Research Finding: **The best way for parents to help their children become better readers is to read to them—even when they are very young. Children benefit most from reading aloud when they discuss stories, learn to identify letters and words, and talk about the meaning of words.**

Comment: The specific skills required for reading come from direct experience with written language. At home, as in school, the more reading the better.

Parents can encourage their children's reading in many ways. Some tutor informally by pointing out letters and words on signs and containers. Others use more formal tools, such as workbooks. But children whose parents simply read to them perform as well as those whose parents use workbooks or have had training in teaching.

The conversation that goes with reading aloud to children is as important as the reading itself. When parents ask children only superficial questions about stories, or don't discuss the stories at all, their children do not achieve as well in reading as the children of parents who ask questions that require thinking and who relate the stories to everyday events. Kindergarten children who know a lot about written language usually have parents who believe that reading is important and who seize every opportunity to act on that conviction by reading to their children.

References: Anderson, R. C., et al. (1985). *Becoming a Nation of Readers: The Report of the Commission on Reading.* Urbana, IL: University of Illinois, Center for the Study of Reading.

Brzeinski, J. E. (1964). "Beginning Reading in Denver." *The Reading Teacher,* Vol. 18, pp. 16-21.

Chomsky, C. (1972). "Stages in Language Development and Reading Exposure." *Harvard Educational Review,* Vol. 42, pp. 1-33.

Dunn, N. E. (1981). "Children's Achievement at School-Entry Age as a Function of Mothers' and Fathers' Teaching Sets." *The Elementary School Journal,* Vol. 81, pp. 245-253.

Heath, S. B. (1983). *Ways with Words: Language, Life and Work in Communities and Classrooms.* New York: Cambridge University Press.

Of course, I thought little of my prescribed lessons, and right here it was greatly to my advantage to have a sensible tutor wise enough to connive at this and other irregularities of the same nature. In this way I ran through Virgil's Aeneid, *then Terence, then Plautus, and some Italian comedies, allured by the pleasure of the subject. On the other hand, had my tutor been so foolish as to deprive me of this amusement, I verily believe I would have brought nothing away from college but a hatred of books, as most of our young gentlemen do.*

Montaigne, 1533-1592
The Education of Children

Independent Reading

Research Finding: **Children improve their reading ability by reading a lot. Reading achievement is directly related to the amount of reading children do in school and outside.**

Comment: Independent reading increases both vocabulary and reading fluency. Unlike using workbooks and performing computer drills, reading books gives children practice in the "whole act" of reading, that is, both in discovering the meanings of individual words and in grasping the meaning of an entire story. But American children do not spend much time reading independently at school or at home. In the average elementary school, for example, children spend just 7 to 8 minutes a day reading silently. At home, half of all fifth graders spend only 4 minutes a day reading. These same children spend an average of 130 minutes a day watching television.

Research shows that the amount of leisure time spent reading is directly related to children's reading comprehension, the size of their vocabularies, and the gains in their reading ability. Clearly, reading at home can be a powerful supplement to classwork. Parents can encourage leisure reading by making books an important part of the home, by giving books or magazines as presents, and by encouraging visits to the local library.

Another key to promoting independent reading is making books easily available to children through classroom libraries. Children in classrooms that have libraries read more, have better attitudes about reading, and make greater gains in reading comprehension than children in classrooms without libraries.

References:

Allington, R. L. (1984). "Oral Reading." In P. D. Pearson (Ed.), *Handbook of Reading Research*, (pp. 829-864). New York: Longman.

Anderson, R. C., et al. (1985). *Becoming a Nation of Readers: The Report of the Commission on Reading.* Urbana, IL: University of Illinois, Center for the Study of Reading.

Dishaw, M. (1977). *Descriptions of Allocated Time to Content Areas for the A-B Period.* San Francisco: Far West Regional Laboratory for Educational Research and Development. Beginning Teacher Evaluation Study Tech. Note IV-11a.

Fielding, L. G., Wilson, P. T., and Anderson, R. C. (in press). "A New Focus on Free Reading: The Role of Trade Books in Reading Instruction." In T. E. Raphael and R. Reynolds (Eds.), *Contexts of Literacy.* New York: Longman.

Heintze, R. A., and Hodes, L. (1981). *Statistics Of Public School Libraries/Media Centers, Fall 1978.* Washington, D.C.: National Center for Education Statistics.

It is befitting, then, Glaucon, that this branch of learning should be prescribed by our law and that we should induce those who are to share the highest functions of state to enter upon that study of calculation and take hold of it, not as amateurs, but to follow it up until they attain to the contemplation of the nature of number by pure thought,...for facilitating the conversion of the soul itself from the world of generation to essence and truth.

Plato, 428-348 B.C.
The Republic, Book VII

Counting

Research Finding:

A good way to teach children simple arithmetic is to build on their informal knowledge. This is why learning to count everyday objects is an effective basis for early arithmetic lessons.

Comment: Young children are comfortable with numbers; "math anxiety" comes in later years. Just watching the enjoyment children get from songs and nursery rhymes that involve counting is ample evidence of their natural ease. These early counting activities can set the stage for later, more formal exposure to arithmetic.

But counting is not limited to merely reciting strings of numbers. It also includes matching numbers to objects and reaching totals (for example, counting the number of apples sitting on the table). Children learn to do arithmetic by first mastering different counting strategies, beginning with rote counting (1,2,3,4), and progressing to memorized computations ($2 \times 2 = 4$). As children learn the facts of arithmetic, they also learn to combine those facts by using more sophisticated strategies. As their skills grow, they rely less and less on counting.

When teachers begin by using children's informal knowledge, then proceed to more complex operations, children learn more readily and enjoy it.

References:

Carpenter, T. P., and Moser, J. M. (1983). "The Acquisition of Addition and Subtraction Concepts." In R. Lesh and M. Landau (Eds.), *Acquisition of Mathematical Concepts and Processes.* New York: Academic Press.

Fuson, K. C., Richards, J., and Briars, D. J. (1982). "The Acquisition and Elaboration of the Number Word Sequence." In C. J. Brainerd (Ed.), *Children's Logical and Mathematical Cognition.* New York: Springer-Verlag.

Gelman, R., and Gallistel, C. R. (1978). *The Child's Understanding of Numbers.* Cambridge: Harvard University Press.

Ginsburg, H. P. (1977). *Children's Arithmetic: The Learning Process.* New York: D. Van Nostrand Company.

Resnick, L. B. (1983). "A Developmental Theory of Number Understanding." In H. P. Ginsburg (Ed.), *The Development of Mathematical Thinking,* (pp. 109-151). New York: Academic Press.

Early Writing

Research Finding: **Children who are encouraged to draw and scribble "stories" at an early age will later learn to compose more easily, more effectively, and with greater confidence than children who do not have this encouragement.**

Comment: Even toddlers, who can hardly hold a crayon or pencil, are eager to "write" long before they acquire the skills in kindergarten that formally prepare them to read and write.

Studies of very young children show that their carefully formed scrawls have meaning to them, and that this writing actually helps them develop language skills. Research suggests that the best way to help children at this stage of their development as writers is to respond to the ideas they are trying to express.

Very young children take the first steps toward writing by drawing and scribbling or, if they cannot use a pencil, they may use plastic or metal letters on a felt or magnetic board. Some preschoolers may write on toy typewriters; others may dictate stories into a tape recorder or to an adult, who writes them down and reads them back. For this reason, it is best to focus on the intended meaning of what very young children write, rather than on the appearance of the writing.

Children become more effective writers when parents and teachers encourage them to choose the topics they write about, then leave them alone to exercise their own creativity. The industriousness of such children has prompted one researcher to comment that they "violate the child labor laws."

References:

Applebee, A. N. (1980). *A Study of Writing in the Secondary School.* Urbana, IL: National Council of Teachers of English. ERIC Document No. ED 197347.

Applebee, A. N. (1984). *Contexts for Learning to Write: Studies of Secondary School Instruction.* Norwood, NJ: Ablex.

Graves, D. H. (1983). *Writing: Teachers and Children at Work.* Exeter, NH: Heinemann Educational Books.

Harste, J. C., et al. (1983). *The Young Child as Writer/Reader, and Informant.* ERIC Document No. ED 234413.

Walshe, R. D. (Ed.) (1981). *Donald Graves in Australia—"Children Want to Write."* Roselle, New South Wales: Primary English Teaching Association.

Speaking and Listening

Research Finding: **A good foundation in speaking and listening helps children become better readers.**

Comment: When children learn to read, they are making a transition from spoken to written language. Reading instruction builds on conversational skills: the better children are at using spoken language, the more successfully they will learn to read written language. To succeed at reading, children need a basic vocabulary, some knowledge of the world around them, and the ability to talk about what they know. These skills enable children to understand written material more readily.

Research shows a strong connection between reading and listening. A child who is listening well shows it by being able to retell stories and repeat instructions. Children who are good listeners in kindergarten and first grade are likely to become successful readers by the third grade. Good fifth-grade listeners are likely to do well on aptitude and achievement tests in high school.

Parents and teachers need to engage children in thoughtful discussions on all subjects—current events, nature, sports, hobbies, machines, family life, and emotions—in short, on anything that interests children. Such discussions should not be limited to reading selections that are part of classwork.

Conversing with children about the world around them will help them reflect on past experiences and on what they will see, do, and read about in the future.

Speaking English at school is especially important for children who have not grown up speaking English.

References: Anderson, R. C., et al. (1985). *Becoming a Nation of Readers: The Report of the Commission on Reading.* Urbana, IL: University of Illinois, Center for the Study of Reading.

Atkin, R., et al. (1977). "Cross-lagged Panel Analysis of Sixteen Cognitive Measures at Four Grade Levels." *Child Development,* Vol. 48, No. 3, pp. 944-952.

Bagford, J. (1968). "Reading Readiness Scores and Success in Reading." *The Reading Teacher,* Vol. 21, No. 4, pp. 324-328.

Humphreys, L. G., and Davey, T. C. (1983). *Anticipation of Gains in General Information: A Comparison of Verbal Aptitude, Reading Comprehension, and Listening.* (Tech. Rep. No. 282). Urbana, IL: University of Illinois, Center for the Study of Reading.

Lohnes, P. R., and Gray, M. M. (1972). "Intelligence and the Cooperative Reading Studies." *Reading Research Quarterly,* Vol. 7, No. 3, pp. 466-476.

Developing Talent

Research Finding: **Many highly successful individuals have above-average but not extraordinary intelligence. Accomplishment in a particular activity is often more dependent upon hard work and self-discipline than on innate ability.**

Comment: High academic achievers are not necessarily born "smarter" than others, nor do people born with extraordinary abilities necessarily become highly accomplished individuals. Parents, teachers, coaches, and the individuals themselves can influence how much a mind or talent develops by fostering self-discipline and encouraging hard work. Most highly successful individuals have above-average but not exceptional intelligence. A high IQ seems less important than specializing in one area of endeavor, persevering, and developing the social skills required to lead and get along well with others.

Studies of accomplished musicians, athletes, and historical figures show that when they were children, they were competent, had good social and communication skills, and showed versatility as well as perseverance in practicing their skill over long periods. Most got along well with their peers and parents. They constantly nurtured their skills. And their efforts paid off.

Developing talent takes effort and concentration. These, as much as nature, are the foundation for success.

References: Bloom, B. S. (Ed.). (1985). *Developing Talent in Young People.* New York: Ballantine Books.

Bloom, B. S., and Sosniak, L. A. (November 1981). "Talent Development vs. Schooling." *Educational Leadership,* Vol. 39, No. 2, pp. 86-94.

Simon, H. A. (1969). *Sciences of the Artificial.* Cambridge: MIT Press.

Walberg, H. J. (September 1969). "A Portrait of the Artist and Scientist as Young Men." *Exceptional Children,* Vol. 36, No. 1, pp. 5-11.

Walberg, H. J. (Spring 1983). "Scientific Literacy and Economic Productivity in International Perspective." *Daedalus,* Vol. 112, No. 2, pp. 1-28.

Ideals

*Research
Finding:* **Belief in the value of hard work, the importance of personal responsibility, and the importance of education itself contributes to greater success in school.**

Comment: The ideals that children hold have important implications for their school experiences. Children who believe in the value of hard work and responsibility and who attach importance to education are likely to have higher academic achievement and fewer disciplinary problems than those who do not have these ideals. They are also less likely to drop out of school. Such children are more likely to use their out-of-school time in ways that reinforce learning. For example, high school students who believe in hard work, responsibility, and the value of education spend about 3 more hours a week on homework than do other students. This is a significant difference since the average student spends only about 5 hours a week doing homework.

Parents can improve their children's chances for success by emphasizing the importance of education, hard work, and responsibility, and by encouraging their children's friendships with peers who have similar values. The ideals that students, their parents, and their peers hold are more important than a student's socioeconomic and ethnic background in predicting academic success.

References: Alexander, C. N., Jr., and Campbell, E. Q. (1964). "Peer Influences on Adolescent Educational Aspirations and Attainments." *American Sociological Review,* Vol. 29, pp. 568-575.

Etzioni, A. (1984). *Self-discipline, Schools, and the Business Community.* Final Report to the U.S. Chamber of Commerce, Washington, D.C. ERIC Document No. ED249-335.

Ginsburg, A., and Hanson, S. (1985). *Values and Educational Success Among Disadvantaged Students.* Final Report to the U.S. Department of Education, Washington, D.C.

Hanson, S., and Ginsburg, A. (1985). *Gaining Ground: Values and High School Success.* Final Report to the U.S. Department of Education, Washington, D.C.

Walberg, H. J. (1984). "Improving the Productivity of America's Schools." *Educational Leadership,* Vol. 41, No. 8, pp. 19-27.

CLASSROOM

When a superior man knows the causes which make instruction successful, and those which make it of no effect, he can become a teacher of others. Thus in his teaching, he leads and does not drag; he strengthens and does not discourage; he opens the way but does not conduct to the end without the learner's own efforts. Leading and not dragging produces harmony. Strengthening and not discouraging makes attainment easy. Opening the way and not conducting to the end makes the learner thoughtful. He who produces such harmony, easy attainment, and thoughtfulness may be pronounced a skillful teacher.

Confucius, c. 550-478 B.C.
Book XVI—*HSIO KI* (*Record on the Subject of Education*)

Getting Parents Involved

*Research
Finding:* **Parental involvement helps children learn more effectively.
Teachers who are successful at involving parents in their
children's schoolwork are successful because they work at it.**

Comment: Most parents want to be involved with their children's schoolwork but are
unsure of what to do or how to do it. Many say they would welcome more
guidance and ideas from teachers. But it takes more than occasional
parent-teacher conferences and school open houses to involve parents.
Teachers who are successful at promoting parent participation in the early
grades use strategies like these:
- Some teachers ask parents to read aloud to the child, to listen to the
  child read, and to sign homework papers.
- Others encourage parents to drill students on math and spelling and to
  help with homework lessons.
- Teachers also encourage parents to discuss school activities with their
  children and suggest ways parents can help teach their children at home.
  For example, a simple home activity might be alphabetizing books;
  a more complex one would be using kitchen supplies in an elementary
  science experiment.
- Teachers also send home suggestions for games or group activities
  related to the child's schoolwork that parent and child can play together.

Teachers meet parents' wishes for face-to-face contact by inviting them to
the classroom to see how their children are being taught. This first-hand
observation shows parents how the teacher teaches and gives parents ideas
on what they can do at home.

References: Becker, H. J., and Epstein, J. (November 1982). "Parent Involvement: A Survey of Teacher Practices." *The Elementary School Journal*, Vol. 83, No. 2, pp. 85-102.

Cattermole, J., and Robinson, N. (September 1985). "Effective Home/School/Communications—From the Parents' Perspective." *Phi Delta Kappan*, Vol. 67, No. 1, pp. 48-50.

Rich, D. K. (1985). *The Forgotten Factor in School Success—the Family.* Washington, D.C.: Home and School Institute.

Walberg, H. J. (February 1984). "Families as Partners in Educational Productivity." *Phi Delta Kappan*, Vol. 65, No. 16, pp. 397-400.

**Reading proficiency tests for 9-,
13-, and 17-year-olds show that:**

- Six percent of 9-year-olds in 1984 could not follow brief written directions or select phrases to describe pictures. Failure to perform these rudimentary reading exercises places them in danger of future school failure.

- Forty percent of 13-year-olds and 16 percent of 17-year-olds attending high school have not acquired intermediate reading skills. They are unable to search for specific information, interrelate ideas, or make generalizations about literature, science, and social studies materials. Inability to perform these tasks raises the question of how well these students can read the range of academic material they are likely to encounter in school.

- Just 5 percent of students at age 17 have advanced reading skills and strategies that enable them to synthesize and restructure ideas presented in specialized or complicated texts used by professional and technical workers.

SOURCE: U.S. Department of Education, National Center for Education Statistics, National Assessment of Educational Progress. (1985). *The Reading Report Card.*

Phonics

Research Finding: **Children get a better start in reading if they are taught phonics. Learning phonics helps them to understand the relationship between letters and sounds and to "break the code" that links the words they hear with the words they see in print.**

Comment: Until the 1930's and 1940's, most American children learned to read by the phonics method, which stresses the relationships between spoken sounds and printed letters. Children learned the letters of the alphabet and the sounds those letters represent. For several decades thereafter, however, the "look-say" approach to reading was dominant: children were taught to identify whole words in the belief that they would make more rapid progress if they identified whole words at a glance, as adults seem to. Recent research indicates that, on the average, children who are taught phonics get off to a better start in learning to read than children who are not taught phonics.

Identifying words quickly and accurately is one of the cornerstones of skilled reading. Phonics improves the ability of children both to identify words and to sound out new ones. Sounding out the letters in a word is like the first tentative steps of a toddler: it helps children gain a secure verbal footing and expand their vocabularies beyond the limits of basic readers.

Because phonics is a reading tool, it is best taught in the context of reading instruction, not as a separate subject to be mastered. Good phonics strategies include teaching children the sounds of letters in isolation and in words (s/i/t), and how to blend the sounds together (s-s-i-i-t).

Phonics should be taught early but not over-used. If phonics instruction extends for too many years, it can defeat the spirit and excitement of learning to read. Phonics helps children pronounce words approximately, a skill they can learn by the end of second grade. In the meantime, children can learn to put their new phonics skills to work by reading good stories and poems.

References: Anderson, R. C., et al. (1985). *Becoming a Nation of Readers: The Report of the Commission on Reading.* Urbana, IL: University of Illinois, Center for the Study of Reading.

Becker, W. C., and Gersten, R. (1982). "A Follow-up of Follow-Through: The Later Effects of the Direct Instruction Model on Children in Fifth and Sixth Grades." *American Educational Research Journal,* Vol. 19, No. 1, pp. 75-92.

Chall, J. S. (1983). *Learning to Read: The Great Debate* (2nd ed.). New York: McGraw-Hill.

Perfetti, C. A., and Lesgold, A. M. (1979). "Coding and Comprehension in Skilled Reading and Implications for Reading Instruction." In L. B. Resnick and P. A. Weaver (Eds.), *Theory and Practice of Early Reading,* Vol. 1, pp. 57-84. Hillsdale, NJ: Erlbaum Associates.

Smith, N. B. (1965). *American Reading Instruction: Its Development and Its Significance in Gaining a Perspective on Current Practices in Reading.* Newark, DE: International Reading Association.

Reading Comprehension

Research Finding: **Children get more out of a reading assignment when the teacher precedes the lesson with background information and follows it with discussion.**

Comment: Young readers, and poor readers of every age, do not consistently see connections between what they read and what they already know. When they are given background information about the principal ideas or characters in a story before they read it, they are less apt to become sidetracked or confused and are more likely to understand the story fully. Afterwards, a question-and-answer discussion session clarifies, reinforces, and extends their understanding.

Good teachers begin the day's reading lesson by preparing children for the story to be read—introducing the new words and concepts they will encounter. Many teachers develop their own introductions or adapt those offered in teachers' manuals.

Such preparation is like a road map: children need it because they may meet new ideas in the story and because they need to be alerted to look for certain special details. Children who are well prepared remember a story's ideas better than those who are not.

In the discussion after the reading lesson, good teachers ask questions that probe the major elements of the story's plot, characters, theme, or moral. ("Why did Pinocchio's nose grow? Why did he lie? What did his father think about his lying? Did their feelings for each other change?") Such questions achieve two purposes: they check students' understanding of what they have just read, and they highlight the kind of meanings and ideas students should look for in future reading selections. These questions also lay the groundwork for later appreciation of the elements of literature such as theme and style. When children take part in a thought-provoking discussion of a story, they understand more clearly that the purpose of reading is to get information and insight, not just to decode the words on a page.

References: Beck, I. L., McCaslin, E. S., and McKeown, M. G. (1981). "Basal Readers' Purpose for Story Reading: Smoothly Paving the Road or Setting Up a Detour?" *The Elementary School Journal*, Vol. 81, No. 3, pp. 156-161.

Durkin, D. (1983). *Is There a Match Between What Elementary Teachers Do and What Basal Reader Manuals Recommend?* Urbana, IL: University of Illinois, Center for the Study of Reading. Reading Ed. Rep. No. 44. ERIC Document No. ED 235470.

Hansen, J. (1981). "The Effects of Inference Training and Practice on Young Children's Reading Comprehension." *Reading Research Quarterly*, Vol. 16, No. 3, pp. 391-417.

Mason, J. (1983). "An Examination of Reading Instruction in Third and Fourth Grades." *The Reading Teacher*, Vol. 36, No. 9, pp. 906-913.

Mason, J., and Osborn, J. (1983). *When Do Children Begin "Reading to Learn"?: A Survey of Classroom Reading Instruction Practices in Grades Two Through Five.* Urbana, IL: University of Illinois, Center for the Study of Reading. Tech. Rep. No. 261. ERIC Document No. ED 220805.

Science Experiments

Research Finding: **Children learn science best when they are able to do experiments, so they can witness "science in action."**

Comment: Reading about scientific principles or having a teacher explain them is frequently not enough. Cause and effect are not always obvious, and it may take an experiment to make that clear. Experiments help children actually see how the natural world works.

Scientific explanations sometimes conflict with the way students may suppose that things happen or work. For example, most students would probably think that a basketball will fall faster than a ping-pong ball because the basketball is larger and heavier. Unless a teacher corrects this intuitive assumption by having the students perform an experiment and see the results, the students will continue to trust their intuition, even though the textbook or the teacher tells them the effect of gravity on both objects is exactly the same and that both will reach the floor at the same instant.

Many students have misconceptions even after taking a science course because they have not had opportunities to test and witness the evidence that would change their minds. To clear up misconceptions, students need to be given the chance to predict the results they anticipate in an experiment. For example, the mistaken idea that the basketball will fall faster than the ping-pong ball can be tested experimentally. The teacher can then explain why the original hypothesis was faulty. In this way experiments help students use the scientific method to distinguish facts from opinions and misconceptions.

References: Champagne, A., and Klopfer, L. (1984). "Research in Science Education: The Cognitive Psychology Perspective." In D. Holdzkom and P. Lutz (Eds.), *Research Within Reach: Science Education.* Charleston, WV: Appalachia Educational Laboratory, Research and Development Interpretation Service. ERIC Document No. ED 247148.

Gentner, D., and Stevens, A. L. (Eds.). (1983). *Mental Models.* Hillsdale, NJ: Erlbaum Associates.

Gunstone, R., and White, R. (1981). "Understanding of Gravity." *Science Education,* Vol. 65, pp. 291-299.

McCloskey, M., Caramazza, A., and Green, B. (1980). "Curvilinear Motion in the Absence of External Forces: Naive Beliefs about the Motion of Objects." *Science,* Vol. 210, pp. 1139-1141.

For the young are not able to distinguish what is and what is not allegory, but whatever opinions are taken into the mind at that age are wont to prove indelible and unalterable. For which reason, maybe, we should do our utmost that the first stories that they hear should be so composed as to bring the fairest lessons of virtue to their ears.

Plato, 428-348 B.C.
The Republic, Book II

Let the Lessons for Reading be varied, that the youth may be made acquainted with good Stiles of all Kinds in Prose and Verse, and the proper Manner of reading each Kind. Sometimes a well told Story, a Piece of a Sermon, a General's Speech to his Soldiers, a Speech in a Tragedy, some Part of a Comedy, an Ode....But let such Lessons for Reading be chosen, as contain some useful Instruction, whereby the Understandings or Morals of the Youth, may at the same Time be improv'd.

Benjamin Franklin, 1706-1790
Autobiography and Other Writings

Storytelling

Research Finding: **Telling young children stories can motivate them to read. Storytelling also introduces them to cultural values and literary traditions before they can read, write, and talk about stories by themselves.**

Comment: Elementary school teachers can introduce young students to the study of literature by telling them fairy tales such as the *Three Billy Goats Gruff* or *Beauty and the Beast* and myths such as *The Iliad*. Even students with low motivation and weak academic skills are more likely to listen, read, write, and work hard in the context of storytelling.

Stories from the oral tradition celebrate heroes who struggle to overcome great obstacles that threaten to defeat them. Children are neither bored nor alienated by learning literature through storytelling; they enjoy, understand, and sympathize naturally with the goats on the bridge, Beauty in a lonely castle, and Hector and Achilles outside the walls of Troy. With the help of skillful questioning, they can also learn to reflect on the deeper meanings of these stories.

Children also benefit from reading stories aloud and from acting out dramatic narrations, whether at home or at school. Parents can begin reading to their children as infants and continue for years to come.

Storytelling can ignite the imaginations of children, giving them a taste of where books can take them. The excitement of storytelling can make reading and learning fun and can instill in children a sense of wonder about life and learning.

References: Applebee, A. N. (1978). *The Child's Concept of Story: Ages Two to Seventeen.* Chicago: University of Chicago Press.

Baker, A., and Greene, E. (1977). *Storytelling: Art and Technique.* New York: R. R. Bowker Co.

Bettelheim, B. (1975). *The Uses of Enchantment: The Meaning and Importance of Fairy Tales.* New York: Alfred A. Knopf.

Cook, E. (1969). *The Ordinary and the Fabulous: An Introduction to Myths, Legends and Fairy Tales for Teachers and Storytellers.* Cambridge and New York: Cambridge University Press.

Sawyer, R. (1962, Revised Edition). *The Way of the Storyteller.* New York: The Viking Press.

Thach, E. (June 1980). "Storytelling: Classics of the Oral Tradition." Report to the National Endowment for the Humanities, Washington, D.C.

To improve the Youth in Composition, they may now, besides continuing to write Letters, begin to write little Essays in Prose, and sometimes in Verse, not to make them Poets, but for this Reason, that nothing acquaints a Lad so speedily with Variety of Expression, as the Necessity of finding such Words and Phrases as will suit with the Measure, Sound, and Rhime of Verse, and at the same time well express the Sentiment.

Benjamin Franklin, 1706-1790
Autobiography and Other Writings

Teaching Writing

Research Finding: **The most effective way to teach writing is to teach it as a process of brainstorming, composing, revising, and editing.**

Comment: Students learn to write well through frequent practice. A well-structured assignment has a meaningful topic, a clear sense of purpose, and a real audience. Good writing assignments are often an extension of class reading, discussion, and activities; not isolated exercises.

An effective writing lesson contains these elements:
- *Brainstorming*: Students think and talk about their topics. They collect information and ideas, frequently much more than they will finally use. They sort through their ideas to organize and clarify what they want to say.
- *Composing*: Students compose a first draft. This part is typically time-consuming and hard, even for very good writers.
- *Revising*: Students re-read what they have written, sometimes collecting responses from teachers, classmates, parents, and others. The most useful teacher response to an early draft focuses on what students are trying to say, not the mechanics of writing. Teachers can help most by asking for clarification, commenting on vivid expressions or fresh ideas, and suggesting ways to support the main thrust of the writing. Students can then consider the feedback and decide how to use it to improve the next draft.
- *Editing*: Students then need to check their final version for spelling, grammar, punctuation, other writing mechanics, and legibility.

Prompt feedback from teachers on written assignments is important. Students are most likely to write competently when schools routinely require writing in all subject areas, not just in English class.

References:

Elbow, P. (1981). *Writing With Power: Techniques for Mastering the Writing Process.* New York: Oxford University Press.

Emig, J. (1971). *The Composing Processes of Twelfth Graders.* Urbana, IL: National Council of Teachers of English. NCTE Research Rep. No. 13. ERIC Document No. ED 058205.

Graves, D. H. (1978). *Balance the Basics: Let Them Write.* New York: The Ford Foundation. ERIC Document No. ED 192364.

Graves, D. H. (1983). *Writing: Teachers and Children at Work.* Exeter, NH: Heinemann.

Hillcocks, G., Jr. (November 1984). "What Works in Teaching Composition: A Meta-Analysis of Experimental Treatment Studies." *American Journal of Education*, Vol. 93, No. 1, pp. 133-170.

Humes, A. (1981). *The Composing Process: A Summary of the Research.* Austin, TX: Southwest Regional Laboratory. ERIC Document No. ED 222925.

Average Mathematics Score for Students in the Eighth Grade: 1981–82

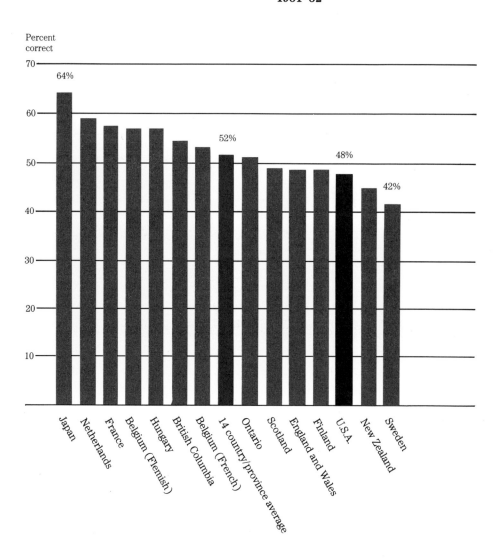

Percent correct

SOURCE: U.S. Department of Education, National Center for Education Statistics. (1985). *Second International Mathematics Study.*

Learning Mathematics

Children in early grades learn mathematics more effectively when they use physical objects in their lessons.

Comment: Numerous studies of mathematics achievement at different grade and ability levels show that children benefit when real objects are used as aids in learning mathematics. Teachers call these objects "manipulatives."

Objects that students can look at and hold are particularly important in the early stages of learning a math concept because they help the student understand by visualizing. Students can tie later work to these concrete activities.

The type or design of the objects used is not particularly important; they can be blocks, marbles, poker chips, cardboard cutouts—almost anything. Students do as well with inexpensive or homemade materials as with costly, commercial versions.

The cognitive development of children and their ability to understand ordinarily move from the concrete to the abstract. Learning from real objects takes advantage of this fact and provides a firm foundation for the later development of skills and concepts.

References: Carmody, L. (1970). "A Theoretical and Experimental Investigation into the Role of Concrete and Semi-Concrete Materials in the Teaching of Elementary School Mathematics." Ph.D. Dissertation, Ohio State University, Columbus.

Fennema, E. (1972). "The Relative Effectiveness of a Symbolic and a Concrete Model in Learning a Selected Mathematical Principle." *Journal for Research in Mathematics Education*, Vol. 3, No. 4, pp. 233-238.

Jamison, D., Suppes, P., and Wells, S. (1974). "The Effectiveness of Alternative Instructional Media: A Survey." *Review of Educational Research*, Vol. 44, No. 1, pp. 1-67.

Piaget, J. (1952). *The Child's Conception of Numbers*. London: Routledge and Kegan Paul.

Suydam, M., and Higgins, J. (1977). "Activity-based Learning in Elementary School Mathematics: Recommendations from Research." Columbus, OH: ERIC Clearinghouse on Science, Mathematics and Environmental Education. ERIC Document No. ED 144840.

Score in Algebra and Calculus for Top 5 Percent of 12th Graders: 1981–82

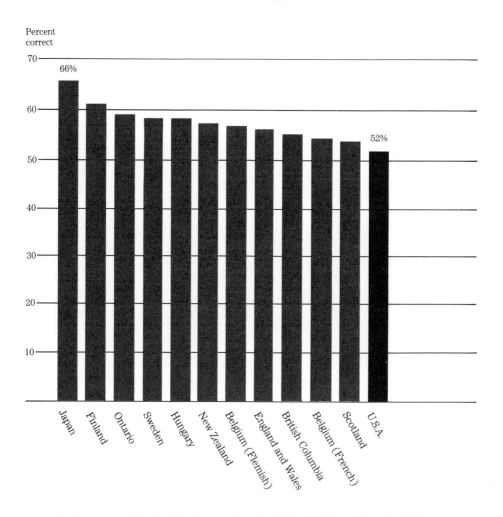

Percent correct

SOURCE: U.S. Department of Education, National Center for Education Statistics. (1985). *Second International Mathematics Study.*

Estimating

Research Finding: **Although students need to learn how to find exact answers to arithmetic problems, good math students also learn the helpful skill of estimating answers. This skill can be taught.**

Comment: Many people can tell almost immediately when a total seems right or wrong. They may not realize it, but they are using a math skill called estimating.

Estimating can also be valuable to children learning math.

When students can make good estimates of the answer to an arithmetic problem, it shows they understand the problem. This skill leads them to reject unreasonable answers and to know whether they are "in the ballpark."

Research has identified three key steps used by good estimators; these can be taught to all students:
- Good estimators begin by altering numbers to more manageable forms—by rounding, for example.
- They change parts of a problem into forms they can handle more easily. In a problem with several steps, they may rearrange the steps to make estimation easier.
- They also adjust two numbers at a time when making their estimates. Rounding one number higher and one number lower is an example of this technique.

Before students can become good at estimating, they need to have quick, accurate recall of basic facts. They also need a good grasp of the place value system (ones, tens, hundreds, etc.).

Estimating is a practical skill; for example, it comes in very handy when shopping. It can also help students in many areas of mathematics and science that they will study in the future.

References: Bestgen, B., et al. (1980). "Effectiveness of Systematic Instruction on Attitudes and Computational Estimation Skills of Preservice Elementary Teachers." *Journal for Research in Mathematics Education*, Vol. 11, pp. 124-136.

Reed, S. K. (1984). "Estimating Answers to Algebra Word Problems." *Journal of Experimental Psychology: Learning, Memory and Cognition*, Vol. 10, pp. 778-790.

Reys, R., et al. (1982). "Processes Used by Good Computational Estimators." *Journal for Research in Mathematics Education*, Vol. 13, pp. 183-201.

Schoen, H. L., et al. (1981). "Instruction in Estimating Solutions of Whole Number Computations." *Journal for Research in Mathematics Education*, Vol. 12, pp. 165-178.

Trafton, P. R. (1978). "Estimation and Mental Arithmetic: Important Components of Computation." In *Developing Computational Skills, 1978 Yearbook*. Reston, VA: National Council of Teachers of Mathematics.

Teacher Expectations

Research Finding: **Teachers who set and communicate high expectations to all their students obtain greater academic performance from those students than teachers who set low expectations.**

Comment: The expectations teachers have about what students can and cannot learn may become self-fulfilling prophecies. Students tend to learn as little—or as much—as their teachers expect.

Students from whom teachers expect less are treated differently. Such students typically:
- are seated farther away from the teacher,
- receive less direct instruction,
- have fewer opportunities to learn new material, and
- are asked to do less work.

Teachers also call on these students less often and the questions they ask are more likely to be simple and basic than thought-provoking. Typically, such students are given less time to respond and less help when their answers are wrong. But when teachers give these same students the chance to answer more challenging questions, the students contribute more ideas and opinions to class discussions.

References:

Brophy, J. E. (1981). "Teacher Praise: A Functional Analysis." *Review of Education Research*, Vol. 51, pp. 5-32.

Good, T. L. (December 1982). "How Teachers' Expectations Affect Results." *American Education*, Vol. 18, No. 10, pp. 25-32.

Good, T. L., and Brophy, J. E. (1984). *Looking In Classrooms* (3rd edition). New York: Harper and Row.

Morine-Dershimer, G. (Winter 1983). "Instructional Strategy and the Creation of Classroom Status." *American Educational Research Journal*, Vol. 20, No. 4, pp. 645-661.

Purkey, S., and Smith, M. (March 1983). "Effective Schools: A Review." *The Elementary School Journal*, Vol. 83, No. 4, pp. 427-452.

Student Ability and Effort

Research Finding: **Children's understanding of the relationship between being smart and hard work changes as they grow.**

Comment: When children start school, they think that ability and effort are the same thing; in other words, they believe that if they work hard they will become smart. Thus, younger children who fail believe this is because they didn't try hard enough, not because they have less ability.

Because teachers tend to reward effort in earlier grades, children frequently concentrate on working hard rather than on the quality of their work. As a result, they may not learn how to judge how well they are performing.

In later elementary grades, students slowly learn that ability and effort are not the same. They come to believe that lower ability requires harder work to keep up and that students with higher ability need not work so hard. At this stage, speed at completing tasks replaces effort as the sign of ability; high levels of effort may even carry the stigma of low ability.

Consequently, many secondary school students, despite their ability, will not expend the effort needed to achieve their potential. Underachievement can become a way of life.

Once students begin believing they have failed because they lack ability, they tend to lose hope for future success. They develop a pattern of academic hopelessness and stop trying. They see academic obstacles as insurmountable and devote less effort to learning.

Teachers who are alert to these beliefs in youngsters will keep their students motivated and on task. They will also slowly nudge their students toward the realism of judging themselves by performance. For example, teachers will set high expectations and insist that students put forth the effort required to meet the school's academic standards. They will make sure slower learners are rewarded for their progress and abler students are challenged according to their abilities.

References: Doyle, W. (1983). "Academic Work." *Review of Educational Research*, Vol. 53, No. 2, pp. 159-199.

Harari, O., and Covington, M. V. (1981). "Reactions to Achievement Behavior From a Teacher and Student Perspective: A Developmental Analysis." *American Educational Research Journal*, Vol. 18, No. 1, pp. 15-28.

Stipek, D. (1981). "Children's Perceptions of Their Own and Their Classmates' Ability." *Journal of Educational Psychology*, Vol. 73, No. 3, pp. 404-410.

Weiner, B. (1979). "A Theory of Motivation for Some Classroom Experiences." *Journal of Educational Psychology*, Vol. 71, pp. 3-25.

Weinstein, R., et al. (1982). "Student Perceptions of Differential Teacher Treatment in Open and Traditional Classrooms." *Journal of Educational Psychology*, Vol. 74, pp. 678-692.

Managing Classroom Time

Research Finding: **How much time students are actively engaged in learning contributes strongly to their achievement. The amount of time available for learning is determined by the instructional and management skills of the teacher and the priorities set by the school administration.**

Comment: Teachers must not only know the subjects they teach, they must also be effective classroom managers. Studies of elementary school teachers have found that the amount of time the teachers actually used for instruction varied between 50 and 90 percent of the total school time available to them.

Effective time managers in the classroom do not waste valuable minutes on unimportant activities; they keep their students continuously and actively engaged. Good managers perform the following time-conserving functions:
- *Planning Class Work*: choosing the content to be studied, scheduling time for presentation and study, and choosing those instructional activities (such as grouping, seatwork, or recitation) best suited to learning the material at hand;
- *Communicating Goals*: setting and conveying expectations so students know what they are to do, what it will take to get a passing grade, and what the consequences of failure will be;
- *Regulating Learning Activities*: sequencing course content so knowledge builds on itself, pacing instruction so students are prepared for the next step, monitoring success rates so all students stay productively engaged regardless of how quickly they learn, and running an orderly, academically focused classroom that keeps wasted time and misbehavior to a minimum.

When teachers carry out these functions successfully and supplement them with a well-designed and well-managed program of homework, they can achieve three important goals:
- They capture students' attention.
- They make the best use of available learning time.
- They encourage academic achievement.

References:

Berliner, D. (September 1983). "The Executive Functions of Teaching." *The Instructor*, Vol. 93, No. 2, pp. 28-40.

Brophy, J. (1979) "Teacher Behavior and Its Effects." *Journal of Educational Psychology*, Vol. 71, No. 6, pp. 733-750.

Hawley, W., and Rosenholtz, S. with Goodstein, H. and Hasselbring, T. (Summer 1984). "Good Schools: What Research Says About Improving Student Achievement." *Peabody Journal of Education*, Vol. 61, No. 4.

Stallings, J. (1980). "Allocated Academic Learning Time Revisited, or Beyond Time on Task." *Educational Researcher*, Vol. 9, No. ll, pp. ll-16.

Walberg, H. J. (1984). "What Makes Schooling Effective? A Synthesis and a Critique of Three National Studies." *Contemporary Education: A Journal of Reviews*, Vol. l, No. l, pp. 22-34.

Direct Instruction

Research Finding: **When teachers explain exactly what students are expected to learn, and demonstrate the steps needed to accomplish a particular academic task, students learn more.**

Comment: The procedure stated above is called "direct instruction." It is based on the assumption that knowing how to learn may not come naturally to all students, especially to beginning and low-ability learners. Direct instruction takes children through learning steps systematically, helping them see both the purpose and the result of each step. In this way, children learn not only a lesson's content but also a method for learning that content.

The basic components of direct instruction are:
- setting clear goals for students and making sure they understand those goals,
- presenting a sequence of well-organized assignments,
- giving students clear, concise explanations and illustrations of the subject matter,
- asking frequent questions to see if children understand the work, and
- giving students frequent opportunities to practice what they have learned.

Direct instruction does not mean repetition. It does mean leading students through a process and teaching them to use that process as a skill to master other academic tasks. Direct instruction has been particularly effective in teaching basic skills to young and disadvantaged children, as well as in helping older and higher ability students to master more complex materials and to develop independent study skills.

References: Berliner, D., and Rosenshine, B. (1976). *The Acquisition of Knowledge in the Classroom.* San Francisco: Far West Laboratory for Educational Research and Development.

Doyle, W. (1985). "Effective Secondary Classroom Practices." In R. M. J. Kyle (Ed.), *Reaching for Excellence: An Effective Schools Sourcebook.* Washington, D.C.: U.S. Government Printing Office.

Good, T., and Grouws, D. (1981). *Experimental Research in Secondary Mathematics Classrooms: Working with Teachers.* Columbia, MO: University of Missouri.

Hansen, J. (1981). "The Effects of Inference Training and Practice on Young Children's Reading Comprehension." *Reading Research Quarterly,* Vol. 16, No. 3, pp. 391-417.

Rosenshine, B. (1983). "Teaching Functions in Instructional Programs." *Elementary School Journal,* Vol. 83, No. 4, pp. 335-351.

Tutoring

Research Finding: **Students tutoring other students can lead to improved academic achievement for both student and tutor, and to positive attitudes toward coursework.**

Comment: Tutoring programs consistently raise the achievement of both the students receiving instruction and those providing it. Peer tutoring, when used as a supplement to regular classroom teaching, helps slow and underachieving students master their lessons and succeed in school. Preparing and giving the lessons also benefits the tutors themselves because they learn more about the material they are teaching.

Of the tutoring programs that have been studied, the most effective include the following elements:
- highly structured and well-planned curricula and instructional methods,
- instruction in basic content and skills (grades 1-3), especially in arithmetic, and
- a relatively short duration of instruction (a few weeks or months).

When these features were combined in the same program, the students being tutored not only learned more than they did without tutoring, they also developed a more positive attitude about what they were studying. Their tutors also learned more than students who did not tutor.

References: Cohen, P. A., Kulik, J. A., and Kulick, C-L. C. (Summer 1982). "Educational Outcomes of Tutoring: A Meta-Analysis of Findings." *American Educational Research Journal*, Vol. 19, No. 2, pp. 237-248.

Devin-Sheehan, L., Feldman, R. S., and Allen, V. L. (1976). "Research on Children Tutoring Children: A Critical Review." *Review of Educational Research*, Vol. 46, No. 3, pp. 355-385.

Mohan, M. (1972). *Peer Tutoring as a Technique for Teaching the Unmotivated.* Fredonia, NY: State University of New York Teacher Education Research Center. ERIC Document No. ED 061154.

Rosenshine, B., and Furst, N. (1969). *The Effects of Tutoring Upon Pupil Achievement: A Research Review.* Washington, D.C.: U.S. Department of Education. ERIC Document No. ED 064462.

Memorization

Research Finding: **Memorizing can help students absorb and retain the factual information on which understanding and critical thought are based.**

Comment: Most children at some time memorize multiplication tables, the correct spelling of words, historical dates, and passages of literature such as the poetry of Robert Frost or the sonnets of Shakespeare. Memorizing simplifies the process of recalling information and allows its use to become automatic. Understanding and critical thought can then build on this base of knowledge and fact. Indeed, the more sophisticated mental operations of analysis, synthesis, and evaluation are impossible without rapid and accurate recall of bodies of specific knowledge.

Teachers can encourage students to develop memory skills by teaching highly structured and carefully sequenced lessons, with frequent reinforcement for correct answers. Young students, slow students, and students who lack background knowledge can benefit from such instruction.

In addition, teachers can teach "mnemonics," that is, devices and techniques for improving memory. For example, the mnemonic "Every Good Boy Does Fine" has reminded generations of music students that E, G, B, D, and F are the notes to which the lines on a treble staff correspond. Mnemonics helps students remember more information faster and retain it longer. Comprehension and retention are even greater when teachers and students connect the new information being memorized with previous knowledge.

References: Anderson, L., Evertson, C. M., and Brophy, J. E. (1979). "An Experimental Study of Effective Teaching in First-grade Reading Groups." *The Elementary School Journal*, Vol. 79, No. 4, pp. 193-223.

Bellezza, F. (1981). "Mnemonic Devices: Classification, Characteristics, and Criteria." *Review of Educational Research*, Vol. 51, No. 2, pp. 247-275.

Carlson, R. F., et al. (January 1976). "Spontaneous Use of Mnemonics and Grade Point Average." *The Journal of Psychology*, Vol. 92, first half, pp. 117-122.

Gregg, L. (Ed.). (1972). *Cognition in Learning and Memory*. New York: John Wiley and Sons.

Rosenshine, B. V. (1983). "Teaching Functions in Instructional Programs." *The Elementary School Journal*, Vol. 83, No. 4, pp. 335-351.

Questioning

Research Finding: **Student achievement rises when teachers ask questions that require students to apply, analyze, synthesize, and evaluate information in addition to simply recalling facts.**

Comment: Even before Socrates, questioning was one of teaching's most common and most effective techniques. Some teachers ask hundreds of questions, especially when teaching science, geography, history, or literature.

But questions take different forms and place different demands on students. Some questions require only factual recall and do not provoke analysis. For example, of more than 61,000 questions found in the teacher guides, student workbooks, and tests for 9 history textbooks, more than 95 percent were devoted to factual recall. This is not to say that questions meant to elicit facts are unimportant. Students need basic information to engage in higher level thinking processes and discussions. Such questions also promote class participation and provide a high success rate in answering questions correctly.

The difference between factual and thought-provoking questions is the difference between asking: "When did Lincoln deliver the Gettysburg Address?" and asking: "Why was Lincoln's Gettysburg Address an important speech?" Each kind of question has its place, but the second one intends that the student analyze the speech in terms of the issues of the Civil War.

Although both kinds of questions are important, students achieve more when teachers ask thought-provoking questions and insist on thoughtful answers. Students' answers may also improve if teachers wait longer for a response, giving students more time to think.

References: Berliner, D. C. (1984). "The Half-Full Glass: A Review of Research on Teaching." In P. L. Hosford (Ed.), *Using What We Know About Teaching.* Alexandria, VA: Association for Supervision and Curriculum Development.

Brophy, J., and Evertson, C. M. (1976). *Learning from Teaching: A Developmental Perspective.* Boston, MA: Allyn and Bacon.

Redfield, D. L., and Rousseau, E. W. (1981). "A Meta-Analysis of Experimental Research on Teacher Questioning Behavior." *Review of Educational Research*, Vol. 51, No. 2, pp. 237-245.

Rowe, M. B. (1974). "Wait-Time and Rewards as Instructional Variables: Their Influence on Language, Logic, and Fate Control: Part One—Wait-Time." *Journal of Research in Science Teaching*, Vol. 11, No. 2, pp. 81-94.

Trachtenberg, D. (1974). "Student Tasks in Text Material: What Cognitive Skills Do They Tap?" *Peabody Journal of Education*, Vol. 52, No. 1, pp. 54-57.

Study Skills

Research Finding: **The ways in which children study influence strongly how much they learn. Teachers can often help children develop better study skills.**

Comment: Research has identified several study skills used by good students that can be taught to other students. Average students can learn how to use these skills. Low-ability students may need to be taught when, as well as how, to use them.

Here are some examples of sound study practices:
- Good students adjust the way they study according to several factors:
  — the demand of the material,
  — the time available for studying,
  — what they already know about the topic,
  — the purpose and importance of the assignment, and
  — the standards they must meet.
- Good students space learning sessions on a topic over time and do not cram or study the same topic continuously.
- Good students identify the main idea in new information, connect new material to what they already know, and draw inferences about its significance.
- Good students make sure their study methods are working properly by frequently appraising their own progress.

When low-ability and inexperienced students use these skills, they can learn more information and study more efficiently.

References: Bransford, J. D. (1979). *Human Cognition: Learning, Understanding and Remembering.* Belmont, CA: Wadsworth.

Brown, A. L., and Smiley, S. S. (1978). "The Development of Strategies for Studying Texts." *Child Development*, Vol. 49, pp. 1076-1088.

Craik, F. I. M., and Watkins, M. J. (1973). "The Role of Rehearsal in Short-Term Memory." *Journal of Verbal Learning and Verbal Behavior*, Vol. 12, pp. 599-607.

Hayes-Roth, B., and Goldin, S. E. (1980). *Individual Differences in Planning Processes.* Santa Monica, CA: The Rand Corporation.

Segal, J., Chipman, S., and Glaser, R. (1985). *Thinking and Learning Skills, Vol. 1: Relating Instruction to Research.* Hillsdale, NJ: Erlbaum Associates.

**Test Scores of 1982 Seniors in
Reading, Science, and Mathematics
by Amount of Homework per Week**

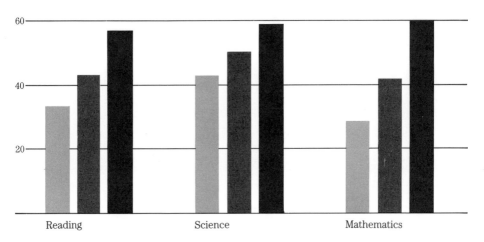

Percent Correct

Subject Areas

- Less than 1 hour
- 1 to less than 5 hours
- 5 or more hours

SOURCE: U.S. Department of Education, National Center for Education Statistics. (1985). *Condition of Education, 1985.*

Homework: Quantity

Research Finding: **Student achievement rises significantly when teachers regularly assign homework and students conscientiously do it.**

Comment: Extra studying helps children at all levels of ability. One research study reveals that when low-ability students do just 1 to 3 hours of homework a week, their grades are usually as high as those of average-ability students who do not do homework. Similarly, when average-ability students do 3 to 5 hours of homework a week, their grades usually equal those of high-ability students who do no homework.

Homework boosts achievement because the total time spent studying influences how much is learned. Low-achieving high school students study less than high achievers and do less homework. Time is not the only ingredient of learning, but without it little can be achieved.

Teachers, parents, and students determine how much, how useful, and how good the homework is. On average, American teachers say they assign about 10 hours of homework each week—about 2 hours per school day. But high school seniors report they spend only 4 to 5 hours a week doing homework, and 10 percent say they do none at all or have none assigned. In contrast, students in Japan spend about twice as much time studying outside school as American students.

References: Coleman, J. S., Hoffer, T., and Kilgore, S. (1982). *High School Achievement: Public, Catholic and Private Schools Compared.* New York: Basic Books.

Keith, T. Z. (April 1982). "Time Spent on Homework and High School Grades: A Large-Sample Path Analysis." *Journal of Educational Psychology*, Vol. 74, No. 2, pp. 248-253.

National Center for Education Statistics. (April 1983). *School District Survey of Academic Requirements and Achievement.* Washington, D.C.: U.S. Department of Education, Fast Response Survey Systems. ERIC Document No. ED 238097.

Rohlen, T. P. (1983). *Japan's High Schools.* Berkeley, CA: University of California Press.

Walberg, H. J. (1984). "Improving the Productivity of America's Schools." *Educational Leadership*, Vol. 41, No. 8, pp. 19-36.

Homework: Quality

Research Finding: **Well-designed homework assignments relate directly to classwork and extend students' learning beyond the classroom. Homework is most useful when teachers carefully prepare the assignment, thoroughly explain it, and give prompt comments and criticism when the work is completed.**

Comment: To make the most of what students learn from doing homework, teachers need to give the same care to preparing homework assignments as they give to classroom instruction. When teachers prepare written instructions and discuss homework assignments with students, they find their students take the homework more seriously than if the assignments are simply announced. Students are more willing to do homework when they believe it is useful, when teachers treat it as an integral part of instruction, when it is evaluated by the teacher, and when it counts as a part of the grade.

Assignments that require students to think, and are therefore more interesting, foster their desire to learn both in and out of school. Such activities include explaining what is seen or read in class; comparing, relating, and experimenting with ideas; and analyzing principles.

Effective homework assignments do not just supplement the classroom lesson; they also teach students to be independent learners. Homework gives students experience in following directions, making judgments and comparisons, raising additional questions for study, and developing responsibility and self-discipline.

References: Austin, J. (1976). "Do Comments on Mathematics Homework Affect Student Achievement?" *School Science and Mathematics*, Vol. 76, No. 2, pp. 159-164.

Coulter, F. (1980). "Secondary School Homework: Cooperative Research Study Report No. 7." ERIC Document No. ED 209200.

Dick, D. (1980). "An Experimental Study of the Effects of Required Homework Review Versus Review on Request Upon Achievement." ERIC Document No. ED 194320.

Featherstone, H. (February 1985). "Homework." *The Harvard Education Letter.*

Walberg, H. J. (April 1985). "Homework's Powerful Effects on Learning." *Educational Leadership*, Vol. 42, No. 7, pp. 76-79.

Assessment

Research Finding:

Frequent and systematic monitoring of students' progress helps students, parents, teachers, administrators, and policymakers identify strengths and weaknesses in learning and instruction.

Comment:

Teachers find out what students already know and what they still need to learn by assessing student work. They use various means, including essays, quizzes and tests, homework, classroom questions, standardized tests, and parents' comments. Teachers can use student errors on tests and in class as early warning signals to point out and correct learning problems before they worsen. Student motivation and achievement improve when teachers provide prompt feedback on assignments.

Students generally take two kinds of tests: classroom tests and standardized tests. Classroom tests help teachers find out if what they are teaching is being learned; thus, these tests serve to evaluate both student and teacher. Standardized tests apply similar gauges to everyone in a specific grade level. By giving standardized tests, school districts can see how achievement progresses over time. Such tests also help schools find out how much of the curriculum is actually being learned. Standardized tests can also reveal problems in the curriculum itself. For example, a recent international mathematics test showed that U.S. students had encountered only 70 percent of what the test covered.

References:

Freeman, D. J., et al. (1983). "Do Textbooks and Tests Define a National Curriculum in Elementary School Mathematics?" *The Elementary School Journal,* Vol. 83, No. 5, pp. 501-513.

Good, T. L., and Grouws, D. A. (1979). "The Missouri Mathematics Effectiveness Project: An Experimental Study in Fourth Grade Classrooms." *Journal of Educational Psychology,* Vol. 71, No. 3, pp. 355-362.

Rosenshine, B. (1983). "Teaching Functions in Instructional Programs." *The Elementary School Journal,* Vol. 83, No. 4, pp. 335-351.

Rutter, M. (1983). "School Effects on Pupil Progress: Research Findings and Policy Implications." In L. S. Shulman and G. Sykes (Eds.), *Handbook of Teaching and Policy* (pp. 3-41). New York: Longman.

Stallings, J. A., and Kaskowitz, D. (1974). *Follow Through Classroom Observation Evaluation, 1972-73.* Menlo Park, CA: Stanford Research Institute. ERIC Document No. ED 104969.

SCHOOL

Instruction increases inborn worth, and right discipline strengthens the heart.

Horace, 65-8 B.C.
Odes, Book IV, ode 4, 1. 33

Effective Schools

Research Finding: **The most important characteristics of effective schools are strong instructional leadership, a safe and orderly climate, school-wide emphasis on basic skills, high teacher expectations for student achievement, and continuous assessment of pupil progress.**

Comment: One of the most important achievements of education research in the last 20 years has been identifying the factors that characterize effective schools, in particular the schools that have been especially successful in teaching basic skills to children from low-income families. Analysts first uncovered these characteristics when comparing the achievement levels of students from different urban schools. They labeled the schools with the highest achievement as "effective schools."

Schools with high student achievement and morale show certain characteristics:
- vigorous instructional leadership,
- a principal who makes clear, consistent, and fair decisions,
- an emphasis on discipline and a safe and orderly environment,
- instructional practices that focus on basic skills and academic achievement,
- collegiality among teachers in support of student achievement,
- teachers with high expectations that all their students can and will learn, and
- frequent review of student progress.

Effective schools are places where principals, teachers, students, and parents agree on the goals, methods, and content of schooling. They are united in recognizing the importance of a coherent curriculum, public recognition for students who succeed, promoting a sense of school pride, and protecting school time for learning.

References:

Bossert, S. (May 1985). "Effective Elementary Schools." In R. Kyle (Ed.), *Reaching for Excellence: An Effective Schools Sourcebook*, (pp. 39-53). Washington, D.C.: U.S. Government Printing Office.

Corcoran, T. (May 1985). "Effective Secondary Schools." In R. Kyle (Ed.), *Reaching for Excellence: An Effective Schools Sourcebook*, (pp. 71-97). Washington, D.C.: U.S. Government Printing Office.

Doyle, W. (May 1985). "Effective Secondary School Practices." In R. Kyle (Ed.), *Reaching for Excellence: An Effective Schools Sourcebook* (pp. 55-70). Washington, D.C.: U.S. Government Printing Office.

Finn, C. E., Jr. (April 1984). "Toward Strategic Independence: Nine Commandments for Enhancing School Effectiveness." *Phi Delta Kappan*, Vol. 65, No. 8, pp. 513-524.

Purkey, S. C., and Smith, M. S. (March 1983). "Effective Schools: A Review." *The Elementary School Journal*, Vol. 83, No. 4, pp. 427-452.

School Climate

Research Finding: **Schools that encourage academic achievement focus on the importance of scholastic success and on maintaining order and discipline.**

Comment: Good schools focus sharply on learning. In effective schools, the school climate—some call it the "learning environment"—puts academics first. Principals and teachers believe they can make a difference in what students learn. Teachers and students believe each student is capable of making significant academic progress. Students understand and agree that their first priority is to learn.

School activities reinforce these attitudes. Routines discourage disorder and disruptions. Teachers and principals protect the classroom from interruptions. Academic success is expected and rewarded. Public ceremonies honor student achievement.

Incoming students know the school's reputation and experienced students affirm the value placed on learning. Teacher morale is high and turnover is low. When there are openings, principals recruit and select teachers who share the school's goals and standards.

Principals work with teachers, students, parents, and community members to develop the school's learning environment. Once established, that learning environment becomes a durable part of the school's tradition.

References: Basualdo, S. M., and Basualdo, E. A. (1980). "Models to Prevent and Deal with Disruptive Behavior(s) in the Classroom: A Review of the Literature." ERIC Document No. ED 202812.

Brookover, W. B., et al. (1979). *School Systems and Student Achievement: Schools Make a Difference.* New York: Praeger.

Coleman, J. S., Hoffer, T., and Kilgore, S. (1982). *High School Achievement: Public, Catholic and Private Schools Compared.* New York: Basic Books.

Grant, G. (Summer 1981). "The Character of Education and the Education of Character." *Daedalus,* Vol. 110, No. 3, pp. 135-149.

Grant, G. (1985). "Schools That Make an Imprint: Creating a Strong Positive Ethos." In J. H. Bunzel (Ed.), *Challenge to American Schools: The Case for Standards and Values,* (pp. 127-143). New York: Oxford University Press.

Rutter, M., et al. (1979). *Fifteen Thousand Hours: Secondary Schools and Their Effects on Children.* Cambridge: Harvard University Press.

Discipline

Research Finding: **Schools contribute to their students' academic achievement by establishing, communicating, and enforcing fair and consistent discipline policies.**

Comment: For 16 of the last 17 years, the public has identified discipline as the most serious problem facing its schools. Effective discipline policies contribute to the academic atmosphere by emphasizing the importance of regular attendance, promptness, respect for teachers and academic work, and good conduct.

Behavior and academic success go together. In one recent survey, for example, high school sophomores who got "mostly A's" had one-third as many absences or incidents of tardiness per semester as those who got "mostly D's." The same students were 25 times more likely to have their homework done and 7 times less likely to have been in trouble with the law. Good behavior as a sophomore led to better grades and higher achievement as a senior.

The discipline policies of most successful schools share these traits:
• Discipline policies are aimed at actual problems, not rumors.
• All members of the school community are involved in creating a policy that reflects community values and is adapted to the needs of the school.
• Misbehavior is defined. Because not everyone agrees on what behavior is undesirable, defining problems is the first step in solving them. Students must know what kinds of behavior are acceptable and what kinds are not.
• Discipline policies are consistently enforced. Students must know the consequences of misbehavior, and they must believe they will be treated fairly.
• A readable and well-designed handbook is often used to inform parents and students about the school's discipline policy.

References:

Brodinsky, B. (1980). "Student Discipline: Problems and Solutions." AASA Critical Issues Report. Arlington, VA: American Association of School Administrators. ERIC Document No. ED 198206.

DiPrete, T. A. (1981). *Discipline, Order, and Student Behavior in American High Schools.* Chicago: National Opinion Research Center. ERIC Document No. ED 224137.

Duke, D. L., and Jones, V. F. (1983). "Assessing Recent Efforts to Reduce Student Behavior Problems." Paper presented at Annual Meeting of the American Educational Research Association, Montreal, Canada. ERIC Document No. ED 233440.

Goldsmith, A. H. (February 14, 1982). "Codes of Discipline: Developments, Dimensions, Directions." *Education and Urban Society* (pp. 185-195). ERIC Document No. EJ 260932.

Myers, D., et al. (1985). "Student Discipline and High School Performance." Paper presented at the Annual Meeting of the American Education Research Association, Chicago.

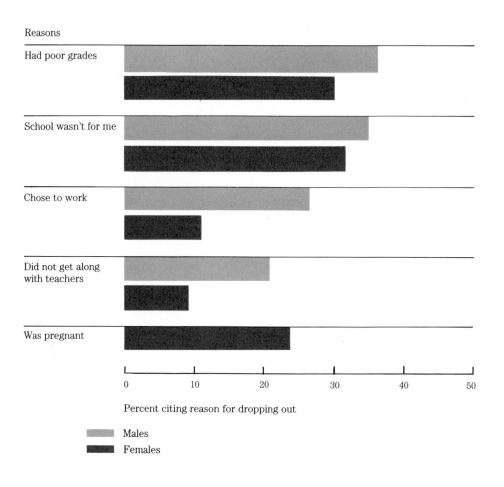

Reasons for Dropping Out of High School, 1982[1]

Reasons

Had poor grades

School wasn't for me

Chose to work

Did not get along with teachers

Was pregnant

0   10   20   30   40   50

Percent citing reason for dropping out

Males
Females

[1] Some students gave multiple reasons for dropping out.

SOURCE: U.S. Department of Education, National Center for Education Statistics. (1983). "High School Dropouts: Descriptive Information from High School and Beyond."

Unexcused Absences

Research Finding: **Unexcused absences decrease when parents are promptly informed that their children are not attending school.**

Comment: Absences are a major problem at all levels of school. Students who miss a lesson lose an opportunity to learn. Too many missed opportunities can result in failure, dropping out of school, or both. Research indicates parents want to hear promptly if their children have poor grades, are creating discipline problems, or have unexcused absences.

Schools have different ways of letting parents know when their children aren't in school. Some use staff members to check attendance records and phone the parents of absent students. Others have begun using automatic calling devices that leave a recorded message with parents. The usual message is a request to contact the school about the absence. These devices can be programmed to call back if no answer is received. Schools using such devices report substantial increases in attendance.

Good attendance in school is another example of the connection of time and learning. Just as homework amplifies learning, regular attendance exposes students to a greater amount of academic content and instruction. Students, of course, must concentrate on their lessons in order to benefit from attendance.

References: Brodinsky, B. (1980). "Student Discipline: Problems and Solutions." AASA Critical Issues Report. Arlington, VA: American Association of School Administrators. ERIC Document No. ED 198206.

Collins, C. H., Moles, O., and Cross, M. (1982). *The Home-School Connection: Selected Partnership Programs in Large Cities.* Boston: Institute for Responsive Education.

deJung, J., and Duckworth, K. (Spring 1985). "Study Looks at Student Absences in High Schools." *Outlook.* Eugene, OR: College of Education, Division of Educational Policy and Management, University of Oregon.

Gotts, E. E. (No Date). "Ways That Effective Home-School Communications Change Across Grade Levels." Charleston, WV: Appalachia Educational Laboratory (mimeographed).

Teacher Supervision

Research Finding: **Teachers welcome professional suggestions about improving their work, but they rarely receive them.**

Comment: When supervisors comment constructively on teachers' specific skills, they help teachers become more effective and improve teachers' morale. Yet, typically, a supervisor visits a teacher's classroom only once a year and makes only general comments about the teacher's performance. This relative lack of specific supervision contributes to low morale, teacher absenteeism, and high faculty turnover.

Supervision that strengthens instruction and improves teachers' morale has these elements:
- agreement between supervisor and teacher on the specific skills and practices that characterize effective teaching,
- frequent observation by the supervisor to see if the teacher is using these skills and practices,
- a meeting between supervisor and teacher to discuss the supervisor's impressions,
- agreement by the supervisor and teacher on areas for improvement, and
- a specific plan for improvement, jointly constructed by teacher and supervisor.

Principals who are good supervisors make themselves available to help teachers. They make teachers feel they can come for help without being branded failures.

References: Bird, T., and Little, J. W. (1985). "Instructional Leadership in Eight Secondary Schools." Final Report to the National Institute of Education. Boulder, CO: Center for Action Research.

Fielding, G. D., and Schalock, H. D. (1985). *Promoting the Professional Development of Teachers and Administrators.* Eugene, OR: ERIC Clearinghouse on Educational Management.

Natriello, G. (1984). "Teachers' Perceptions of the Frequency of Evaluation and Assessments of Their Effort and Effectiveness." *American Educational Research Journal*, Vol. 21, No. 3, pp. 579-595.

Natriello, G., and Dornbusch, S. M. (1981). "Pitfalls in the Evaluation of Teachers by Principals." *Administrator's Notebook*, Vol. 29, No. 6, pp. 1-4.

Wise, A. E., et al. (1984). *Teacher Evaluation: A Study of Effective Practices.* Santa Monica, CA: Rand Corporation. ERIC Document No. ED 246559.

Cultural Literacy

Research Finding: **Students read more fluently and with greater understanding if they have background knowledge of the past and present. Such knowledge and understanding is called cultural literacy.**

Comment: Students' background knowledge determines how well they grasp the meaning of what they read. For example, students read passages more deftly when the passages describe events, people, and places of which the students have some prior knowledge. The more culturally literate students are, the better prepared they will be to read and understand serious books, magazines, and other challenging material.

Most school teachers, college professors, journalists, and social commentators agree that the general background knowledge of American students is too low and getting lower. Surveys document great gaps in students' basic knowledge of geography, history, literature, politics, and democratic principles. Teaching is hindered if teachers cannot count on their students sharing a body of knowledge, references, and symbols.

Every society maintains formal and informal mechanisms to transmit understanding of its history, literature, and political institutions from one generation to the next. A shared knowledge of these elements of our past helps foster social cohesion and a sense of national community and pride.

In the United States, the national community comprises diverse groups and traditions; together they have created a rich cultural heritage. Cultural literacy not only enables students to read better and gain new knowledge; it enables them to understand the shared heritage, institutions, and values that draw Americans together.

References:
Anderson, R. C., Soiro, R. J., and Montague, W. (1977). *Schooling and the Acquisition of Knowledge.* Hillsdale, NJ: Erlbaum Associates.

Finn, C. E., Jr., Ravitch, D., and Roberts, P. (Eds.) (1985). *Challenges to the Humanities.* New York: Holmes and Meier.

Hirsch, E. D., Jr. (Spring 1983). "Cultural Literacy." *The American Scholar,* Vol. 52, pp. 159-169.

Hirsch, E. D., Jr. (Summer 1985). "Cultural Literacy and the Schools." *American Educator,* Vol. 9, No. 2, pp. 8-15.

Levine, A. (1980). *When Dreams and Heroes Died: A Portrait of Today's College Student.* San Francisco: Jossey-Bass, Inc.

Resnick, D. B., and Resnick, L. B. (August 1977). "The Nature of Literacy: An Historical Exploration." *Harvard Educational Review,* Vol. 47, No. 5, pp. 370-385.

This I regard as history's highest function, to let no worthy action be uncommemorated, and to hold out the reprobation of posterity as a terror to evil words and deeds.

Tacitus, 55-118
Annals

For this purpose the reading in the first stage, where they will receive their whole education, is proposed, as has been said, to be chiefly historical. History, by apprising them of the past, will enable them to judge of the future; it will avail them of the experience of other times and other nations; it will qualify them as judges of the actions and designs of men; it will enable them to know ambition under every disguise it may assume; and knowing it, to defeat its views.

Thomas Jefferson, 1743-1826
Notes on Virginia and Other Writings

History

Research Finding:

Skimpy requirements and declining enrollments in history classes are contributing to a decline in students' knowledge of the past.

Comment: Earlier generations of American students commonly learned the history of American institutions, politics, and systems of government, as well as some of the history of Greece, Rome, Europe, and the rest of the world. Today, most States require the study of only American history and other course work in social studies. Indications are that students now know and understand less about history.

In most State requirements for high school graduation, a choice is offered between history on the one hand and courses in social science and contemporary social issues on the other. Most high school students, even those in the academic track, take only one history course. Students enroll in honors courses in history at less than half the rate they enroll for honors courses in English and science. Typically, requirements have also declined for writing essays, producing research-based papers, and reading original sources. Similar declines are reported in the requirements for such reasoning skills as evaluating sources of information, drawing conclusions, and constructing logical arguments.

As a result, students know too little about the past. The National Assessment of Education Progress has pilot-tested the knowledge of 17-year-olds about American history. The preliminary results of this study, due for release in 1987, indicate that two-thirds of the students tested could not place the Civil War within the period 1850-1900; half could not identify Winston Churchill or Stalin.

The decline in the study of history may hinder students from gaining an historical perspective on contemporary life.

References:
Fitzgerald, F. (1979). *America Revised: History School Books in the Twentieth Century.* Boston: Atlantic Little-Brown.

Owings, J. A. (1985). "History Credits Earned by 1980 High School Sophomores Who Graduated in 1982." *High School and Beyond Tabulation.* Washington, D.C.: National Center for Education Statistics.

Ravitch, D. (November 17, 1985). "Decline and Fall of Teaching History." *New York Times Magazine,* pp. 50-52; 101; 117.

Ravitch, D. (1985). "From History to Social Studies." In *The Schools We Deserve: Reflections on the Educational Crisis of Our Times* (pp. 112-132). New York: Basic Books.

Shaver, J. P., Davis, O. L., Jr., and Helburn, S. W. (February 1979). "The Status of Social Studies Education: Impressions from Three NSF Studies." *Social Education,* Vol. 43, No. 2, pp. 150-153.

Thernstrom, S. (1985). "The Humanities and Our Cultural Challenge." In C. E. Finn, D. Ravitch, and P. Roberts (Eds.), *Challenges to the Humanities.* New York: Holmes and Meier.

Percent of High School Students Studying Foreign Language

Percent studying language

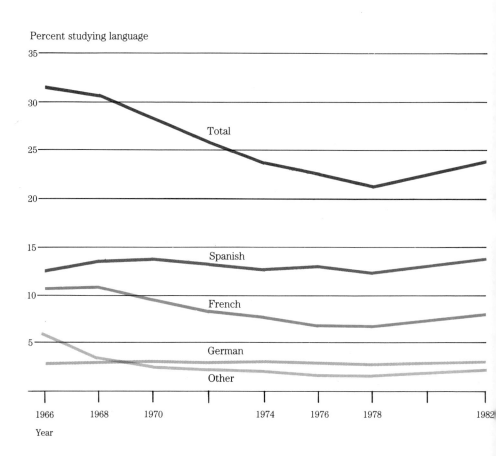

SOURCE: U.S. Department of Education, Center for Statistics (forthcoming). *Digest of Education Statistics, 1985;* and American Council on the Teaching of Foreign Languages, Inc. (1985 unpublished).

Foreign Language

Research Finding:
The best way to learn a foreign language in school is to start early and to study it intensively over many years.

Comment:
The percentage of high school students studying foreign language declined from 73 percent in 1915 to 15 percent in 1979. Some States and schools are beginning to emphasize foreign language study. However, even with this new emphasis, most students who take a foreign language study it for 2 years or less in high school and do not learn to communicate with it effectively.

Students are most likely to become fluent in a foreign language if they begin studying it in elementary school and continue studying it for 6 to 8 years. Although older students may learn foreign languages faster than younger ones, students who start early are likely to become more proficient and to speak with a near-native accent.

"Total immersion" language study programs in the United States and Canada that begin instruction in the early grades and teach all subjects in the foreign language have been highly successful in teaching all students both the language and regular academic subjects.

If new foreign language requirements are really to improve students' language competence, experience has shown that schools will need to:
- find qualified teachers,
- set consistent goals,
- select appropriate materials, and
- continue a coherent program of instruction from elementary to junior to senior high school.

References:
Eddy, P. A. (1981). "The Effect of Foreign Language Study in High School on Verbal Ability as Measured by the Scholastic Aptitude Test-Verbal." Washington, D.C.: Final Report of the Center for Applied Linguistics. ERIC Document No. ED 196312.

Grittner, F. M. (1981). "Teaching Issues in Foreign Language Education: Current Status and Future Directions for Research." Madison, WI: Department of Public Instruction. ERIC Document No. ED 203711.

Hortas, C. R. (1984). "Foreign Languages and Humane Learning." In C. E. Finn, D. Ravitch, and R. T. Fancher (Eds.), *Against Mediocrity: The Humanities in America's High Schools*. New York: Holmes and Meier.

Krashen, S. D., Long, M. A., and Scarella, R. C. (December 1979). "Age, Rate, and Eventual Attainment in Second Language Acquisition." *TESOL Quarterly*, Vol. 13, No. 4, pp. 573-582.

Stern, H. H., and Cummins, J. (1981). "Language/Teaching/Learning Research: A Canadian Perspective on Status and Directions." In J. K. Phillips (Ed.), *Action for the '80's: A Political, Professional, and Public Program for Foreign Language Education*. Skokie, IL: National Textbook Co.

**Percent of 1982 High School
Graduates Who Met Curricular
Recommendations of the National
Commission on Excellence in
Education**

Curricular Recommendations

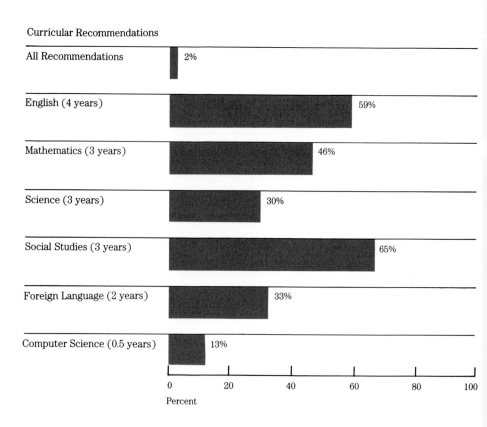

All Recommendations	2%
English (4 years)	59%
Mathematics (3 years)	46%
Science (3 years)	30%
Social Studies (3 years)	65%
Foreign Language (2 years)	33%
Computer Science (0.5 years)	13%

0   20   40   60   80   100

Percent

SOURCE: U.S. Department of Education, National Center for Education Statistics. (1984). *Condition of Education, 1984.*

Rigorous Courses

Research Finding: **The stronger the emphasis on academic courses, the more advanced the subject matter, and the more rigorous the textbooks, the more high school students learn. Subjects that are learned mainly in school rather than at home, such as science and math, are most influenced by the number and kind of courses taken.**

Comment: Students often handicap their intellectual growth by avoiding difficult courses. In order to help young people make wise course choices, schools are increasingly requiring students to take courses that match their grade level and abilities; schools are also seeing to it that the materials used in those courses are intellectually challenging.

The more rigorous the course of study, the more a student achieves, within the limits of his capacity. Student achievement also depends on how much the school emphasizes a subject and the amount of time spent on it: the more time expended, the higher the achievement. Successful teachers encourage their students' best efforts.

References: Chall, J., Conard, S., and Harris, S. (1977). *An Analysis of Textbooks in Relation to Declining SAT Scores.* New York: College Entrance Examination Board.

Ginsburg, A., Baker, K., and Sweet, D. (1981). "Summer Learning and the Effects of Schooling: A Replication of Heyns." Paper presented at the Annual Meeting of the American Educational Research Association, Los Angeles, CA. ERIC Document No. ED 204367.

Holsinger, D. (1982). "Time, Content and Expectations as Predictors of School Achievement in the USA and Other Developed Countries: A Review of IEA Evidence." Paper presented to the National Commission on Excellence in Education, New York. ERIC Document No. ED 227077.

Pallas, A. M., and Alexander, K. L. (Summer 1983). "Sex Differences in Quantitative SAT Performance: New Evidence on the Differential Coursework Hypothesis." *American Educational Research Journal*, Vol. 20, No. 2, pp. 165-182.

Walberg, H. J., and Shanahan, T. (1983). "High School Effects on Individual Students." *Educational Researcher*, Vol. 12, No. 7, pp. 4-9.

Acceleration

Research Finding: **Advancing gifted students at a faster pace results in their achieving more than similarly gifted students who are taught at a normal rate.**

Comment: Advocates of accelerating the education of gifted and talented students believe that this practice furnishes the extra challenge these students need to realize their full potential. Critics believe acceleration may result in emotional and social stress if a child is unable to get along with older students. Some, concerned about those who remain behind, characterize acceleration as unfair or undemocratic.

Research evidence generally supports acceleration. When abler students are moved ahead in school, they typically learn more in less time than students of the same age and ability who are taught at the conventional rate. Accelerated students score a full grade level or more higher on achievement tests than their conventionally placed schoolmates. Some may score several years ahead of their schoolmates.

Acceleration does not damage students' attitudes about school subjects. Nor do accelerated students necessarily become drudges or bookworms; they ordinarily continue to participate in extracurricular activities. Such students often become more sure about their occupational goals.

Accelerated students perform as well as talented but older students in the same grade. Despite being younger, accelerated students are able to capitalize on their abilities and achieve beyond the level available to them had they remained in the lower grade.

References: Cohn, S. J., George, W. C., and Stanley, J. C. (Eds). (1979). "Educational Acceleration of Intellectually Talented Youths: Prolonged Discussion by a Varied Group of Professionals." In W. C. George, S. J. Cohn, and J. E. Stanley (Eds.), *Educating the Gifted: Acceleration and Enrichment*, (pp. 183-238). Baltimore: Johns Hopkins University Press.

Getzels, J. W., and Dillon, J. T. (1973). "The Nature of Giftedness and the Education of the Gifted." In R. M. W. Travers (Ed.), *Second Handbook of Research on Teaching*, (pp. 689-731). Chicago: Rand McNally.

Goldberg, M. (1958). "Recent Research on the Talented." *Teachers' College Record*, Vol. 60, No. 3, pp. 150-163.

Gowan, J., and Demos, G. D. (1964). *The Education and Guidance of the Ablest*. Springfield, IL: Charles C. Thomas.

Kulik, J. A., and Kulik, C. C. (1984). "Synthesis of Research on Effects of Accelerated Instruction." *Educational Leadership*, Vol. 42, No. 2, pp. 84-89.

Extracurricular Activities

Research Finding: **High school students who complement their academic studies with extracurricular activities gain experience that contributes to their success in college.**

Comment: High school class rank and test scores are the best predictors of academic success in college, but involvement sustained over time in one or two extracurricular activities contributes to overall achievement in college. On the other hand, when these activities become ends in themselves, academic performance may suffer.

Students who participate in extracurricular activities gain some significant advantages. Among them are:
- opportunities for recognition, personal success, and broader experience to complement their academic achievement,
- the chance to develop intellectual, social, cultural, and physical talents to round out their academic education, and
- the opportunity to extend the boundaries of the classroom by acquiring direct experience with the content and worth of a subject; for example, when drama club members study and present the plays of Shakespeare, or when debaters gain practice in applied logic, research, and public presentations.

Although such activities as athletics are less clearly related to academic goals, they do provide opportunities for physical growth and self-discipline. Indeed, all these activities can extend the range of experience that schools can offer.

But when extracurricular activities get out of balance, problems can arise, as when high school athletes treat sports as an alternative to learning rather than an addition to it. Distracted by the prestige they earn in sports, student athletes may fail to prepare adequately for the academic requirements of college or the workplace. This situation has worsened in recent years, and many abuses have come to light, such as lowering (or winking at) the academic requirements for sports eligibility. There have been recent attempts to rectify this situation by reinstating academic criteria as a condition for participation in all extracurricular activities.

References: Braddock, J. H., II. (1981). "Race, Athletics, and Educational Attainment." *Youth and Society*, Vol. 12, No. 3, pp. 335-350.

Purdy, D., Eitzen, D. S., and Hufnagel, R. (1982). "Are Athletes Students? The Educational Attainment of College Athletes." *Social Problems*, Vol. 29, No. 4, pp. 439-448.

Spady, W. (1970). "Lament for the Letterman: Effects of Peer Status and Extracurricular Activities on Goals and Achievement." *American Journal of Sociology*, Vol. 75, No. 4, pp. 680-702.

Spady, W. (1971). "Status, Achievement, and Motivation in the American High School." *School Review*, Vol. 79, No. 3, pp. 379-403.

Willingham, W. W. (1985). *Success in College: The Role of Personal Qualities and Academic Ability.* New York: College Board Publications.

Preparation for Work

Research Finding: **Business leaders report that students with solid basic skills and positive work attitudes are more likely to find and keep jobs than students with vocational skills alone.**

Comment: As new technologies make old job skills obsolete, the best vocational education will be solid preparation in reading, writing, mathematics, and reasoning. In the future, American workers will acquire many of their job skills in the workplace, not in school. They will need to be able to master new technologies and upgrade their skills to meet specialized job demands. Men and women who have weak basic skills, or who cannot readily master new skills to keep pace with change, may be only marginally employed over their lifetimes.

Business leaders recommend that schools raise academic standards. They point to the need for remedial programs to help low-achieving students and to reduce dropping out.

Business leaders stress that the school curriculum should emphasize literacy, mathematics, and problem-solving skills. They believe schools should emphasize such personal qualities as self-discipline, reliability, perseverance, teamwork, accepting responsibility, and respect for the rights of others. These characteristics will serve all secondary students well, whether they go on to college or directly into the world of work.

References: Center for Public Resources. (1982). *Basic Skills in the U.S. Work Force: The Contrasting Perceptions of Business, Labor, and Public Education.* New York.

Committee for Economic Development. (1985). *Investing in Our Children: Businesses and the Public Schools: A Statement.* New York and Washington, D.C.

National Academy of Science, National Academy of Engineering, Institute of Medicine, and Committee on Science, Engineering and Public Policy. (1984). *High Schools and the Changing Workplace: The Employer's View.* Washington, D.C.: National Academy Press.

National Advisory Council on Vocational Education. (1984). *Conference Summary: Vocational Education and Training Policy for Today and Tomorrow.* Washington, D.C.

Zemsky, R., and Meyerson, M. (1986). *The Training Impulse.* New York: McGraw Hill.

Now to put into effect all the suggestions which I have given is the province of prayer, perhaps, or exhortation. And even to follow zealously the majority of them demands good fortune and much careful attention, but to accomplish this lies within the capability of man.

Plutarch, 46-120
The Education of Children
(Volume 1 of Plutarch's *Moralia*)

ACKNOWLEDGMENTS

The staff members of the Office of Educational Research and Improvement who helped to identify, frame, evaluate, and winnow the research findings that comprise the core of the report:

Kevin Arundel
Marilyn Binkley
John Blake
Jim Bradshaw
Mamie Brown
Michael Brunner
Ronald Bucknam
the late Stephen Cahir
Phillip Carr
Jo Anne Cassell
Margaret Chavez
Judi Conrad
Clara M. Lawson Copeland
Dennis Cuddy
Alexander Cuthbert
Emerson J. Elliott
Ann Erdman
James N. Fox
Cheryl Garnette
Peter Gerber
Norman Gold
Rene Gonzalez
Barbara Greenberg
Ron Hall
Charles Haughey
Enid Herndon
Laurabeth Hicks
Charlene Hoffman
Jacqueline Jenkins
Milbrey Jones

Dick Jung
Susan Klein
Gerald Kulm
Mary Lewis
Gail MacColl
Suellen Mauchamer
James McGeever
Charles Missar
Oliver Moles
Tetsuo Okada
Ronald Pedone
Ronald Preston
Laura Rendon
Barbara Richardson
Marshall Sashkin
Jeff S. Schiller
Judith W. Segal
Bernice Slaughter
Stephen Sniegoski
Thomas Snyder
Frank Stevens
Anne P. Sweet
John L. Taylor
Oscar Uribe
Joseph Vaughn
Kent Viehover
Patricia Welch
Frank Withrow
Emily Wurtz

ORDERING INFORMATION

Several of the references listed in the bibliography include an ERIC Document Number (ED 000111). This number can be used to order copies of the document from ERIC or to locate the full text of the document in a library with an ERIC microfiche collection.

ERIC, which stands for the Educational Resources Information Center, is a nationwide information system devoted to the field of education. It is designed to provide classroom teachers, students, parents, and policymakers with information about innovative programs and practices in education, conference proceedings, bibliographies, significant speeches, and educational research and development. It is supported by the Office of Educational Research and Improvement of the U.S. Department of Education.

There are more than 700 locations in the United States where ERIC microfiche collections are maintained, including college and public libraries.

To find the nearest ERIC collection, contact:
ERIC Processing and Reference Facility
ORI, Inc., Information Systems Division
4833 Rugby Avenue, Suite 301
Bethesda, Maryland 20814
Telephone: 301/656-9723

To obtain the price of an ERIC document and ordering information, contact:
ERIC Document Reproduction Service
Computer Microfilm Corp.
3900 Wheeler Avenue
Alexandria, Virginia 22304
Telephone: 1-800/227-3742 (toll free)
(In Virginia: 703/823-0500)

To learn more about this report contact our Information Office toll free at 800/424-1616 (in the Washington, D.C. metropolitan area call 463-0083), or write: Information Office, 1200 19th Street, N.W., Washington, D.C. 20208-1403. The Information Office is staffed with statisticians and education and information specialists who can answer questions about education statistics, research, technology, and practices, particularly as they relate to programs in the Office of Educational Research and Improvement.

Additional copies of this report are available from the Consumer Information Center, Pueblo, Colorado 81009.